Flashes of Insight

Gateways to Mindfulness

Michael Forester

First published in Great Britain in 2024

by Paralight Press

www.michaelforester.co.uk

The right of Michael Forester

to be identified as author of this work

has been asserted by him in accordance with

the Copyright, Designs and Patents Act 1988

ISBN: 9781838011444 Paperback

ISBN: 9781838011451 E-Book

PARALIGHT

PRESS

Meditation is to see deeply into things,
to see how we can change,
how we can transform.

Thich Nhat Hahn
Being Peace

Contents

Introduction

In a sound-bite world of tweets and snaps, where do
we turn to find depth? Here are fifty-two gateways to
mindfulness that will each take you about five minutes to
read. They will provoke thought and awareness, drawing
back the curtain of illusion, inviting you to transition
deeper. Read them while you are waiting for a train,
standing in a supermarket queue, when you are early for
an appointment; use them to open a time of meditation.
Read them as they were written: all the way through,
without stopping. Then pause. Allow them to reach you
before you read another. If you want to know how they
came about, continue reading this introduction below.
But that's not what is important. What matters most is
that you read each flash, let it wash over you, then step
through that gateway you have created in doing so, into
mindful awareness.

If you want to know more about how they came to be, this is their story.

In October 2022 I took three weeks out of my schedule to spend on Tenerife on a solo, silent retreat. One of my intentions was to play a series of half-day retreat videos by Henry Shukman[1] on the subject of Samadhi meditation. Henry introduced a number of speakers to his deeply provocative programme, who all brought great insight to the subject. One in particular, a speaker who was new to me, was Natalie Goldberg[2].

Natalie started her discourse by smoothing down her shoulder length grey hair and saying *Look - I now have a hair do instead of a hair don't!* She went on to demonstrate a formidable understanding of the meditation process and some of the obstacles commonly encountered along the way. But it was this first statement more than anything else that intrigued me, for it spoke of someone who had found liberation from the straightjacket of conformity, of a person who had spent a lifetime discovering who she was.

Researching further, I discovered that Natalie is a Zen writing teacher who had written a million copy best seller, *Writing Down The Bones*[3]. Why had I not heard of her before, I wondered. Why was it virtually impossible to lay my hands on this hugely successful book? And for that matter, why would such a book be allowed to go out of print? Finally, I tracked down a second-hand copy of a pocket edition in the United States and had it flown over to the UK where I live. I was not to know that this tiny book, measuring just 11cm by 6cm, was to knock me off my metaphorical feet, and impact profoundly my writing, my meditation practice and my life.

Natalie Goldberg pioneered the use of writing as a meditative practice in its own right and sets out the rules of what she calls Writing Practice:

- Keep your hand moving
- Be specific
- Lose control
- Don't think

Well, I had no option really, did I? I had to employ the system and find out its value for myself. Within days the power of letting go through Writing Practice had become obvious. Within a few more days *Flashes of Insight* was born - five minute reads where the clouds part and the illumination shines through to bring into consciousness what you have always known.

I offer them to you with bowed head. May they illuminate your steps on your own Journey to the Light. May they show you more of who and what you are.

Michael Forester
March 2024

1 Five Ladies

In the queue at the counter of Costa café stand five ladies. The first two, who are together, are dressed for sport – the younger in shorts and sleeveless running top, the slightly older lady in joggers and t-shirt. They collect their coffees and make space at the counter for two older ladies, casually dressed in denim jeans and loose tops. I don't see what they order as my head is down while I type into my screen. Next comes a young woman in t-shirt and white shorts pushing a pushchair. She will enjoy a few minutes breathing space while her baby sleeps. Two years ago, perhaps she would have been dressed in running kit or maybe fashionable skirt and top. Now, with the arrival of her child, life has become more focused on practicalities. Babies throw up on fashionable clothes (and yes, I've had more than one breakfast burped over me in my time). It's easier to wear what is quickly replaceable and less valued.

Much as she needs a coffee break, I'm guessing she values her child more than her break or her clothes. We adapt. We improvise. We adjust to the circumstances in which we find ourselves.

Further down the line is a woman in her forties wearing a long, loose mustard coloured top over striped slacks that are designed, can we say discreetly, to accommodate the fuller figure. Perhaps she too gave birth to children years ago. Before that, perhaps she was a sportswoman in shorts and sleeveless vest. Next comes a portly, balding gentleman of about my own age in white t-shirt and blue shorts. Years ago, he might well have dressed, as did I, in business suit with formal shirt and tie. The business of business still continues but neither of us participates in it any more. What seemed vital twenty or thirty years ago has been unmasked for the passing, impermanent illusion it really is.

I smile more at the world now. Not in a patronising way but with compassion. All phases seem permanent as we pass through them – twenty plus years of child rearing that seemed beyond my energy, business crises that were just a few years or even months long yet seemed eternal, so much did I have invested in my preferred outcome. Political and economic crises, climate emergencies, earthquakes, accidents or fires with tragic, unforeseen consequences: all absorb our attention so completely that the moment seems eternal. Just as it did thirty-six years ago to me when I stared into the face of a prognosis that foretold a life of deafness. Just as it did three hundred and fifty-seven years ago when a fire swept across the wooden buildings of London and raised that powerful city to the ground. Just as it did in Pompeii in AD 79 when Vesuvius exploded without warning and blanketed the city with fire and molten rock. All were events of profound consequence to those affected such that time seemed to stop and suffering seemed interminable. Yet all passed. We adapt. We improvise. We adjust to the circumstances in which we find ourselves.

Today, as you become preoccupied with events, ask yourself what is transient, what is for a lifetime and what is permanent. Then ask yourself what matters. And, oh yes, the young lady in the sleeveless top and shorts has just walked out the door. Perhaps in the next few years she too will become a mother with a pushchair, a lady in her forties in expandable slacks, an elder taking time out to look back on a lifetime, well lived or otherwise.

2 Clutching The Butterfly

There is a ritual to this process: the noting of date and start time at the top of the hand-written draft, the coffee growing cold in the reusable cup, the buttered wholemeal toast not quite finished. And four wrappers from the butter pats left on the plate. Always four. Always returned to the plate after consumption. Then I can start.

It's not that I can't write without all that. It's simply that setting the scene, undertaking the ritual, sets this time apart – sanctifies it if you will, renders it special, some might say holy. The preparatory process slows the mind to concentrate upon the moment. And now the hand is poised upon page, ready to write what comes.

I could be in church at this moment, or temple, in a synagogue, or a Zendo. All places of ritual, all in some sense sacred spaces, set aside from the humdrum and rush. We release our preoccupation with the superficially important to concentrate upon the moment and what dwells in the moment, outside of time, encompassing timing, outside of activity, wrapping its now-ness around the silence.

Here, when the meditation gong sounds, or the priest's voice breaks through the distraction, or the shaman's drum first beats, here is where we return to what we are, as the illusion evaporates. We abandon goals, projects and objectives. We release our attempts to control and discover what happens when there is no control, neither our own nor someone else's in a space where everything is allowed simply to be as it is.

We are dedicated change-makers, we humans, always wanting things to be other than how they are, then grasping onto the impossibility of sustaining what we think we wanted. We change what is, in order to make it suit our preference, then refuse stubbornly to see that the moment we have arrived at cannot be held. We miss the point: that everything changes. Not occasionally, not periodically, but continuously, moment by moment, each in-breath filling the space inside, each out-breath emptying. Then the briefest of pauses when we touch the silence.

Grasp it at your peril. You miss the point if you clutch the butterfly, breaking its wings as you hold it tight in your fist, destroying the very thing you are trying to sustain. There is congruence in opening the palm, knowing that the bright and colourful fluttering thing was never yours to possess. Why attempt the impossibility of ownership, possession, when there is another moment to be entered into? Focus on sustaining the moment that was and you miss the moment that is. Receiving the power of now depends on permitting now to evaporate. A paradox that is not a paradox.

Eventually you see it, of course. However many moments, however many lifetimes it takes, you understand in the end that now is continuous and continuously becoming.

The incense burns down, the candle burns out, the vibrations of the gong wane, all spreading out into what is next.

Why would you be afraid of becoming what you have always been?

3 Waltzing

Have you ever woken and risen before sunrise in mid-summer? Take a moment to see it with me now. At 4.00 am the first hint of dawn is just beginning to appear over the tall oak trees in the copse at the back of the garden. The light is grey, lending the world an eerie hue. But we know that more is to come. We know that the light will rise yet stronger, as inexorably the sun rises and the first bright rays come filtering through the branches. The leaves will start to rustle and the first bird song will herald the day, as the garden comes alive with light. And the glory of this is that no one did anything to make it happen – not even the sun itself. It does not rise or set, it just burns on intensively out there in the void. Not the trees, not the birds, nor the insects, all of which await its daily appearance to get on with the job of creating more life in the endless cycle. The only movement is in the world itself, perpetuating its dizzy spin alongside all those other worlds that turn around this, and all the other suns, relentless dancers, waltzing their way around the universal ballroom, circling, spinning, energy to energy, life to life, cycle to cycle, a tide that rises and falls, breathing in the light and the life, breathing out in sustained rhythm, just like our own biorhythms and circadian rhythms, the rhythms of our history and prehistory, our unwritten and unknown future history.

And I, a dizzy writer, am caught up in that spin with not the first idea of what I am going to write, morning after morning, moment after moment, letting the pen flow, letting the light flow, letting the life flow, until my own last exhalation and my return to centre, power and emptiness. And all of it is seen afresh each day when, and only when, I am prepared to stop trying to control and let go.

4 Diving And Soaring

Yesterday was a difficult day. It didn't start out that way, though. I rose early, read from two personal development books and meditated. All was normal. At least, all was normal until I settled down to work. I had two tasks before me – to analyse the reasons for low profitability at my last sales event despite the high book sales we had achieved and to ensure I was properly prepared for the next event. I examined my records of the weekend's sales closely. But try as I might, I could not see where I had gone wrong. I became frustrated. I became angry with myself for not seeing what should have been obvious – for what would have been obvious years ago when I practised as a chartered accountant. I beat myself up for my lack of perception. I was certain that at the root of it was my own aging process. I don't think so clearly at the age of 68 as I did at 36. *I've got to stop doing this*, I thought. *I'm harming myself.*

So I put the analysis aside and looked at the arrangements I had been sent by the organisers for my next event – a one-day signing in Sherborne. They were a little vague on the subject of where to unload the car and where to park for the day. I emailed the organiser and received an almost instant response – but it wasn't much clearer. So I wrote again and the next response – again instant – didn't do the job either. I began to berate myself again, this time for being deaf and unable to phone her to sort out the problem. By lunchtime I had decided I was the most useless, old, incapable creature to crawl upon God's earth. I poured my energy into mental self-flagellation. I hated myself for my inadequacy. It would be better for all if I was dead.

Extreme? You bet.

But I do that sometimes. Suffice to say, eventually, I found solutions to both problems. But not before I had exhausted myself, wasting my energy on inward focused anger directed at a core belief that I still carry: that I am not good enough.

This morning everything changed. Feeling a little delicate from the previous day's performance, I rose early and sat to meditate. I let everything be as it was and the quiet, blessed peace, descended upon me once again. Twenty or so minutes later I turned to one of my personal development books – Natalie Goldberg's *The True Secret of*

Writing.[4] Today's chapter was on letting go, what I need to let go of to experience the moment as it is.

And then it clicked. I had spent the previous day identifying with feelings, believing those feelings, believing I was what I felt. My mood soared at the revelation until I realised quite suddenly that I was doing it again – this time identifying with positive emotions, the ones we want to cling to.

That was when I saw it: that it was the identification with my feelings, the grasping at them, the attachment and holding onto them, whether positive or negative, that was preventing me from experiencing what actually is in the moment. Since then I have been pondering it, meditating on it, returning to it. So simple, yet so easily missed.

Equanimity lies in letting go of all of it, negative or positive, and simply being, without comment, criticism, or intervention. That is where the moment lies and that is the reality of now.

5 Court Holy Water In A Dry House

At the table next to where I am sitting is a little boy. He seems such a happy soul. He reminds me of a picture I have seen of myself at about the same age – sheer joy on my face as I hold up a bucket of sand on a beach somewhere in Pembrokeshire.

It takes so little to create happiness. Yet we spend our lives pursuing it as if it were some quarry that we have to run to ground. We employ dog packs of activity to pursue it, hoping to corner it in some remote inaccessible location, only to find it has moved on just moments before our arrival. So we pursue it with the next trinket, the next project, the next holiday, angst-laden in our fear that it will always remain one step ahead and will always evade our pursuit. Then comes the time when we drop in exhaustion, somewhere out on a barren moor, as the storms of disappointment deluge their unfair wind and hail upon us. Unfair, because we did everything right, did we not? We played by the rules that were supposed to bring us happiness. Yet here, after years of pursuit, we lie exhausted and empty-handed, facing the reality that the chase to which we gave ourselves was hopeless from the start, the quarry a mere figment of a skilled advertiser's manipulative imagination. If we get lucky, we stop – right there in the middle of the storm. Like King Lear, we seek no shelter as we watch it rage about us, as the endless stream of possessions and activities disperses. We wait, letting the silence rise up from the wells inside us, shifting our perception first fractionally, then radically, letting what is be as it is, waiting as the passion subsides, the storm calms and the illusion evaporates, making space for being to begin.

6 War Zone

I have just completed a three-day Easter event at Lyndhurst, Hampshire. I attend numerous of these small shows. For the most part they are fill-ins between the big county shows and festivals where I usually sign for readers. They are relatively easy, particularly if they are close to home, like this one is.

It was clear from the start that Lyndhurst was going to be uneventful. Good weather and inflation-constrained budgets conspired to keep people outside. But eventually folks start to appear, circling the room and stopping to talk to crafters selling jewellery, or candles, or fudge, or a hundred other offerings you see at such events.

It being holiday time, we also see quite a few visitors from abroad. I always enjoy passing a few words with folk in French or German, if that's their language. Even though deafness prevents me from understanding what is said in return, I find pretty much everyone appreciates it when you reach out to them in their own language. So the hours flowed quite easily and the people flowed round the hall with buoyancy in their energy when the sun shone, or with longer faces when the wind blew and the rain dashed down - it was that kind of weekend weather-wise.

I was there more than anything else to launch my new book, *Forest Pathways*, a collection of inspirational essays, poetry and metaphorical fiction created largely during walks in The New Forest. I had held my breath before launch day. I was hopeful, of course. But a lot of work goes into a new book over several years and you never know until its first unveiling how it will be received. Nevertheless, it sold very well and with each happy buyer I sighed inwardly in contentment, or relief, or both.

I virtually always find there are special people at events like this – people it seems I am almost meant to meet, people who will find a particular book lifechanging. But this weekend it had not happened.

Then came Easter Monday, a surly, sullen day with dark skies and hail, a day for driving home early if ever I saw one. Nevertheless, after a slow start we saw some surges of people between the extended lulls. I didn't think anything of it when a teenage girl, her long dark hair tied back in a band, came towards the table, hanging back a little, not wanting to engage. I don't push for connection if folk don't want it. But she eyed *If It Wasn't For That Dog*, my book about Matt, my now deceased hearing dog, looking at its bright yellow cover and the endearing picture of his spaniel eyes on the front. I picked up a copy and held it out towards her. She didn't make eye contact with me but took hold of the book and looked it over closely, reading the back cover and dipping into the text at random before returning it to the pile then walking away. I moved on to other folk who did want to talk and thought no more about her. Until, that was, she returned to the table a second time and did the same thing again before walking away once more with reluctance in her eyes. I wondered what was happening for her. I wondered why the book was so engaging to this young person. I often feel the energy but normally do not know the detail until the person chooses to disclose. All I can do is be there for those that want to engage, to connect when they reach out to do so.

Finally she returned to the table with her family group, pointed the book out to an older person, a grandmother perhaps. The older lady took £10 from her purse and gave it to the girl, who picked up the book and handed it to me with the money. Holding both, I asked her, *Would you like this dedicated with your name in the front?* She nodded. *What's your name* I asked? She answered in what I took to be a northern European accent – maybe Dutch or Belgian, I thought, but I couldn't hear well enough to be sure. *I need you to write that down for me* I said touching my implant. *Sorry about the deafness.* I smiled at her. She still looked worried and stressed. The name she wrote down and handed to me was Anastasia. I was intrigued. *Where do you come from?* I asked.

Ukraine she answered. It took a moment to sink in. And in the moment of realisation of what that meant, everything changed for me. The full force of the horror of the war hit me: the terror of the explosions, the flight from danger, the crossing of Europe, the struggle to find a sponsor family to live with in the UK. As I looked across the table at her, everything else dissolved around me. How little it mattered whether I had a successful show or not, whether folk bought my books or not. Here was a living example of what matters most in our lives. Here was teenage Anastasia who had lived through horror after horror, whose life would always be affected by what had happened to her, her relatives and her friends. I handed the money straight back to her. Well you would, wouldn't you? *Take any books on the table that you like* I heard myself saying. *There is no charge.*

She took only Matt's book. I don't remember what I said after that. I only remember reaching out to her with my eyes across the table that morning. I only remember wanting her to know that she was safe, that she was loved. And I remember thinking that the special person I was there for the day was not Anastasia. It was me.

7 Defection

I am a dedicated Tesco shopper. Or at least, I used to be. I love the delivery service, the ease of online ordering, the Clubcard points that we trade occasionally for cash vouchers that make the weekly shop seem cheaper. But that was before. Before inflation. Before Aldi came to town.

Then came the day when we could stand for it no longer. There had been too many articles in the online feeds concerning middle-class shoppers defecting from Waitrose (whose revered portals I had not afforded to enter for some time) to Aldi on grounds of cost and the latter's apparent ability to offer comparable quality. If such elevated beings as Waitrose shoppers had migrated to these sunnier climes, who was I, a shopper in the frozen north of Tesco, to argue? Finally, we forewent the ease of the delivery service that had arrived at the kitchen door, courtesy of a cheery-faced driver who made friendly conversation week by week. Instead, we joined the bewildered ranks of virgin trolley-pushers, making their wide-eyed way between the unexpectedly wide aisles and bottom floor prices of Aldi.

There was much they did not offer that we like to buy, so such visits were followed rapidly by guilty commando raids back into our former grocery home to pick up gluten-free oatcakes or sheep's cheese. But this served only to make us note the all-too-obvious fact that we seem to spend the same on one lightly packed bag in Tesco as we had on three bulging, arm-stretching carriers in their price-aggressive competitor across the road.

As penance for such visits, we forced ourselves into Tesco's in-store Costa Coffee franchise and accepted our punishment of coffee and toast as we observed the strange, unenlightened creatures that continued to exit the store with expensively-filled trollies piled high. Our conversion was complete. We were now as confused by this inexplicable behaviour in which we ourselves had so recently indulged as we had once been by those formerly alien creatures that roamed the aisles of Aldi and emerged with their wallets and purses still as full as their trollies.

So what is the learning here, I ask myself? Certainly that thrift is a virtue to be valued above status (not that there was ever much of the latter when shopping in Tesco's, you understand); that we owed no more loyalty to Tesco than they felt towards us, mere cannon fodder of the automated checkout. Rather, that I am intrigued by my own inclination to inertia. I was slow to be convinced that changing from Tesco to Aldi would be worthwhile. But now, just a few weeks later, I have learned the layout of my new preferred grocery retailer and zip round the store, pouncing on offers as fast as any self-respecting seagull dives onto the fish and chips of the unwary seaside holidaymaker.

And thus we come to it: once I have convinced myself of something, once I have settled into a new pattern of behaviour, it becomes difficult to shift me from my repetitions. And therein lies a clue to how to become much more effective at anything I want to do. It takes tenacity. It takes repetition of the desired pattern, even if it is sometimes easier – indeed even if it is significantly easier – to revert to former patterns. I remind myself again of the need for sustained behaviour even when my tired old mind comes up with excuse after excuse for taking the road regularly travelled, even when I do not see the speed of progress for which I was hoping. Because it is by sustaining behaviour through the resistance to change that a new, preferred and better way of being is established – and that is what makes all the difference.

Now, I must ask you to excuse me. Tesco's delivery driver is at the kitchen door.

8 Starship Taoists

In Glastonbury for a five-day break, the possibilities flow easily. There has been no difficulty writing this week, for the subjects present themselves on every street corner – crystal shops and fairy shops, holy thorns and Buddhist temples, folk both young and old who are careful to dress so as not to conform and thereby simply conform to a different norm. The bag lady who seems to live in the car park, her trolley pile so high that it is taller than she is, filled with sleeping bag, carrier bags, empty buckets, and a pink umbrella, all held in place by a tarpaulin tied down by bungee straps. Where she goes, the trolley goes. On the first day of our stay when we walked out at about 9.00 am (the crack of dawn by Glastonbury standards) she was rubbing her eyes awake under the covered area in the car park. By yesterday morning she had moved thirty metres to stand outside the church and by lunchtime a few metres more to stand in the High Street, her trolley blocking most of the pavement. Like everyone else, we walked around her where she stood quietly, non-disruptively, seeking no engagement. Today she must be holding vigil somewhere else, for she has not appeared.

A little further up the High Street, the pavement is chalked with notices that declare 'Crop circles not Covid' and 'Why is the HQ of the EU in Brussels?' In Café Zero where I am writing, a beautiful young woman sits on the squishy brown leather sofa in the window discreetly feeding her baby under a shawl. Over the road in the churchyard, thirty or so people await admission to the church, where Grand Master Mantak Chia[5] offers to unfold the mysteries of the Tao. I find myself wondering if the Tao might be better understood by the baby feeding at her mother's breast.

Even the café itself is very Glastonbury. Spread across the counter are all the usual offerings of cakes and buns and crisps. On the wall behind, the drinks menu lists the usual range of coffee, chocolate and smoothies. But the shiplap boarding on the front of the counter is painted in lime green. The table at which I am writing is carefully covered with sticky-backed plastic sporting blue polka dots, while the one next to it is adorned with cartoon cows coloured in yellow and green. All the cows have red noses. In the corner of the room stands a dog crate containing Skippy, a nine-month old Springer Spaniel (yes, I asked –

of course I asked). Skippy is happy to sleep his day away until the allotted pee-break time arrives when he is led off to the back of the café where, no doubt, there is an outdoor space.

We must vacate this table soon, for the clock is heading towards midday when the lunchtime crowd will arrive, dressed in long skirts and beads, straight from the Buddhist temple, or Enlightenment (that's the singing bowl shop) or Chalice Well – wherever the energy of the ley lines is strongest for them today. The whole alternative world is here. But the Alternatives still want their caramel lattes or their caramel frappes. Even if you are about to catch the next starship to vibrate in the fifth dimension, you still need lunch before you launch. Over the road, Master Mantak Chia must also be winding down for lunch. Perhaps he too will be arriving shortly for his mushroom toastie. We are all Taoists, of course, even if some of us do not realise it.

As we exit the café the beautiful girl has finished feeding her baby, who is now sleeping on the shoulder of an older man with a long grey drooping moustache sitting opposite her. Outside, the bag lady is studying seedlings at a small pop-up plant market, her trolley standing some way off, temporarily forgotten in the importance of the moment. I find myself wondering where she might intend to plant the seedlings in which she is showing so much interest. We proceed up the High Street to Earthfare, the organic grocery store, where a woman dressed in a purple sari and a brown trilby with a large feather is paying for her groceries on Apple Pay. We pay for our organic crackers and probiotic yoghurt then wander back down the hill to a fairy shop where a real live fairy, with fuller figure and undersized gossamer wings on her back, is talking earnestly into her mobile phone with a supplier. I refrain from taking a photo. But later, outside, I will snap Merlin[7] the wizard in the full-length blue robe and pointy hat as he pulls his shopping trolley behind him.

I wonder if the bag lady bought the seedlings. I wonder if the baby in Café Zero will become a starship trooper. Or maybe a Taoist. Perhaps both. But he will definitely have a dog called Skippy.

9 Small Change

Before Writing Practice this morning I visited with my new friend, Maria. Maria is a seller of the Big Issue magazine who stands at her pitch just outside of Morrisons supermarket in the High Street. A few weeks back I gave her my business card as she had shown some interest in my writing. Now she texts me each week to tell me when she will be in town, to ask how I am, or just to tell me how her baby boy is.

Today is a blustery day in New Milton. It's just a few days on from a storm that in some parts of the country dropped a month's worth of rain in less than two hours. It's not raining here yet but the forecast tells me there's a 90% chance of heavy rain from now through until the end of the day.

As I approach, I see that Maria is wrapped up under several layers of clothing. She still looks cold to me. I stop and chat with her for a few minutes. She tells me her little boy is ill with a childhood cold – hopefully, nothing special, but as a mother she would still prefer to be with him than to be standing on a windy street hoping to sell magazines to the occasional shoppers as they proceed in and out of the store. Fighting off the wind with their tightly-wrapped coats, their anxiousness to get into the store means that most either don't notice her or don't take the time to search their pockets for the £4.00 price of the magazine.

As I approach, she sees me and smiles, as is her way. From some yards distant I smile back and bow, as is my way. *How are you?* she asks as I draw closer. I smile as I check my well-being inside before answering. I don't like to make glib responses to this, the most frequent and often the most superficial of greetings. But I am well, centred and happy and I tell her so. *But how is your child?* I ask. *Improving,* she says, *but still not well. I'm only here because I need to buy formula for him.* I note mentally the financial circumstances that must challenge her, such that today's sales are necessary to permit the purchase of today's baby formula.

I know from a previous conversation that she buys the magazines for £2.00 each and sells them at the cover price of £4.00. Not such a bad margin. But not such a good return either, when you have to buy around 25 of them and stand there all day in order to sell them. Last week, she says, between 2.00pm and 5.00pm she sold only two magazines. It's a pattern I know well from selling my books at shows. Sales tend to concentrate in the mornings. Afternoon visitors are fewer and typically spend less.

I find myself wondering, now, how many copies she was left with at the end of that day and how many people paid her just the cover price. Sometimes folk give her an extra pound. That's not too difficult for some of us. You hand over a fiver and don't notice the pound change that never hits your pocket.

Seeing how cold she looks, I ask if she is allowed to take a break and maybe visit the café for some warmth and a drink. *Oh yes*, she says. *But I worry that I will miss buyers. Even eating here on my pitch can be difficult as sometimes people won't stop if I'm chewing.*

How many more magazines do you need to sell in order to buy the formula? I ask. She reckons in her head for a moment. *Only another two or three.* I'm relieved, perhaps visibly so. It's only 10.00am. She'll make those sales quite easily. But I know she'll still stay in her pitch all day anyway. A few more pounds will mean she gets to eat too.

I'm on my way into Morrisons, so I offer to buy her a hot drink. She is a little taken aback but grateful. Shopping completed, I come out balancing a large tea with no milk – there was none on the stand. She has not drunk tea without milk before but she is still grateful. I'm wondering if it might be all she gets today. Hopefully not, though. I have seen others stop and ask her what she would like to eat, then buy her a sandwich.

I give her a note for the magazine. She knows I will not want change. I know it brings that formula a step closer. That's a fair exchange. Then I head off to the café my £4.85 breakfast and Writing Practice. Maria is glad of the conversation and the sale. I am glad of the opportunity to give, to be reminded of what it was like when

too was living hand to mouth, to be reminded of how privileged I am now.

Two-way gain. Two-way blessing. Two-way learning. That's a fair exchange too.

10 Uplifting

So a friend asks me this morning, *What is your purpose in meditating?* It would have been a deeply challenging question if not for the fact that it had occurred to me just a few minutes before, when I was coming to the end of my morning meditation. 'Why am I doing this? What is my outcome?' When I thought about it at some length, I was surprised to come to the conclusion that I had no outcome.

Let me state it clearly: I am not seeking to achieve or change anything when I meditate. And this comes from someone who has lived his whole life in the pursuit of one objective after another. Those objectives were first guided by significant others towards imposed targets: learn to read, aim for top of the class, get your O-levels, get your A-levels, achieve high enough grades to get into a good university, get onto a good career ladder. And when the process of goal-setting had become habitual, there were the goals I set myself: become a partner in an accounting practice by age 30, write a successful business book, establish my own practice, write another book, become a millionaire. One outcome after another, one goal after another.

And then, without warning, all was gone – my hearing, my family, my business, my self-assessed high achievements – the things that made all the other people who admire achievement go *Wow!* I had been adept at pushing aside everything that did not fit the achievement model. Until, that was, depression hit. Depression that was generated by the dishonesty gap between who I felt myself to be inside and who I was projecting myself to be. It sat stubbornly on my shoulders, squashing me so far down into the darkness of self-loathing, that I simply could not pursue any more goals. In fact, I could barely get out of the chair.

I tried therapy (and not for the first time). I was faithful with it for over a year until that too became pointless – it simply wasn't achieving the goal of feeling better.

Why I sought a meditation teacher, I cannot really say. I can only tell you that, when in July 2020, I happened upon Sam Harris' Waking Up App[6], it sat comfortably with me. All that was required of me was 10 minutes of doing nothing each day. Even I could manage that. Mind you, it took me three months to establish it as a daily practice.

And then it became part of my daily routine. Something as natural to me as taking a shower or eating lunch. Something I didn't have to think about prioritising. I lost sight of my original purpose, the stopping of depression. Meditation simply became something that I did. And a year later I turned around and found that depression was no longer ruling my life.

Did the darkness ever come back? Assuredly. And some days were indeed dark, as that voice of self-deprecation perched on my shoulder, whispering into my ear what a loathsome creature I was. Habitually, I would first try to fight it off, then finally believe in it and come almost to love that loathing, making 'poor me' my greatest friend and my saddest, most loved companion. But now something had changed. Not in the attacks of depression themselves but it in what I did with them.

I looked at that voice and found it was just a voice. I looked at the words of worthlessness that it spoke and saw they were vacuous. And I looked at my mind and saw it was made up of thoughts and spaces in between the thoughts. Some were helpful – pick up that cup, stop at that junction, etc. Some were unhelpful – you're too tired to get out of the chair, you're a vile waste of space on the planet, you've got no right to exist. There were still the words of thought, just as before. But now I had learned that I did not have to fill them with meaning beyond themselves. I did not have to believe them. And how did

I stop believing them? Well, it was obvious. They were all just thought and I had learned that all thought is empty. As I continued to practice and formal meditation sessions became longer, I began to understand that there was more to meditation than the awareness that brought freedom from depression. There was a whole lot more. There was vastly, inestimably more. And I rather think we will be exploring some of that in future Flashes.

But for now, it is what it is, and it is enough.

11 On Bogeymen And Sandmen

I'm back in Costa café this morning, reading the newspaper online, reluctant to start Writing Practice, just like I used to be reluctant to meditate. Looking at why I feel this way is itself challenging, because it makes me confront fear – and when I am afraid I would rather look away. Fear, I know, is just another appearance in consciousness, just another pattern of energy to which I have given a name.

Eventually, the names that we give things become more frightening than the phenomena themselves: 'the bogyman will get you' strikes fear, though as children we are never at all clear what it is that we fear. If the bogeyman has a face, it comes from cinematographic nightmares rather than real nightmares, from the ill-chosen strategies our parents employed to persuade us to sleep when we were little. Though how we are to sleep when we have been induced to fear is never made clear. Why is it that we are taught to fear the bogeyman but to love the Sandman, when neither have a face we have ever seen?

Next come our teenage years, when we are chided for our love of the Sandman and threatened with all manner of undesirable consequences if we submit to his charms to rise late and arrive at school after the bell has rung. Indeed, some of us at that age were told that we have become the Bogeyman – or will do so if we do not mend our ways. Of course by this point the versatile Bogeyman has been rechristened Mr Failure, Mr Worthless, Mr Unfulfilled-Potential.

Eventually comes the inaptly named Adulthood – though how many of us are actually adults when we reach the age of legal majority is a highly debatable matter. The Bogeyman goes by other names now – Mr Unreasonable Boss, Mrs Demanding Wife, Miss Enticing Liaison. Where sleeps the Sandman now? Often he is nowhere to be seen as we toss the night away, disturbed in dream and sleeplessness alike by images of such personas as the Bogeyman has chosen as his next incarnation. Mr Sandman will have to wait as we strive our lives away, gyrating to the pipes of Mr Bogeyman, wondering how we ever allowed ourselves to be conscripted into his dance troupe. *I'll sleep when I'm dead*, Clive Owen declares in the movie of the same name. We nod in admiration, wishing we, too, were disdainful of fear and inactivity. Yet the more we suppress them, the harder they call, until we heed, or die, or age enough to look back on an unsatisfied life and wonder how it came to be.

So, at the end of that life and at the end of this piece I return to my awareness that fear is just an energy pattern to which I have given a name, be that 'Bogeyman' or 'What Might Happen.' I write for my designated twenty minutes and have learned a little more about how to conquer the Bogeyman. But tonight, when I retire, I might still take a quick glance under the bed.

12 Prompt

Today I asked my writing partner, Jacqui, for a writing prompt (did you think I did this Writing Practice alone?). Whatever your passion, whatever your art, the purpose of a prompt is the equivalent of priming a pump – to get the flow to commence.

Throw a bucket of water over a pump and you can use that pump to draw water from the well. Though our wells run deep and we are brim full of creativity from the source within, sometimes the rains are delayed. The water table falls low. It can be painful and sore to tap into waters that run so deep. So we prime the pump and let the water trickle down, lubricating the dry, dusty pipework until the connection to the subterranean aquifers has been re-established. Then we pump. We pump hard and with determination. We work that pump relentlessly – not in desperation or despair but in the certainty that the waters will come; that in doing our part of tenacious, relentless pumping, we know that up will flow the sweet water. We do not worry about its quality, for we know there is no brackish poison here. We are tapping into the wellsprings of our common soul, the waters of eternity, the lubrication of spirit that brings life to a thirsty land. Let it gush forth, let it pour forth, work through that resistance. Ignore the dour voices that say 'No point, no hope', that deny the possibility of water. Those feelings of hopelessness have power only if you believe them, only if you turn them into an excuse for the inactivity of despondency. Break through them and your emotions turn into your allies, your servants, as you pump and pump in the determination of certainty that the water is there, that the land needs it and you are charged with the responsibility of drawing it forth, libation to the thirsty, liberation to the bound, light to the darkened.

For such is the nature of this water that lies in measureless depths beneath the surface of the mirage that is our presenting life. Pump on until you see through it to uncover what is real. For it is then that the illusion itself dematerialises and all that is left is the water, the water of love that brings life to a thirsty land.

13 Iron Road

Well, it's obvious isn't it?

And yet so often it is not. Even when we think we understand something because it's staring us in the face, so to speak, it turns out repeatedly that we have not understood.

Our thinking runs on railway lines. We set our expectations of the future straight out in front of us based on our perceptions of the past. We think that because something happened a particular way before it's going to do the same again. Because I learned that this gesture, this look, this action meant something once, I proceed on the presumption that it is going to do so now and forever. That iron road stretches forward inexorably, cutting its unwavering furrow through the ground before us, stretching as far into the future as we can imagine. And so our minds, those clunking iron horses, run forward on their guide rails, never distracted by possibility, never seeing the alternative, never permitting us to see past the illusion that is our perceived certainty.

Until, that is, something lies before us that we have not encountered before: a boulder too big to be dislodged. At first the engine of our mind chugs forward, pushing itself against the immovable rock in its path. But all the horsepower, all the steam, all the heat of effort that we can muster will not move it. So we back up a bit. We take a run at it. We smash ourselves against it in the certainty that it's not really there. It's just a mirage shimmering in the desert. And however hard we try, we can't push and shove that tired old engine of our minds through the boulder. But still we won't let go of the reassurance that those rails offer us. They've seen us through every crisis of our short little lives so they must be right, mustn't they? They kept us on message all this time, so if we just go on repeating the same mantras of belief as we always did, then surely this boulder will evaporate and we will see those rails stretching forward to the horizon just as we expect to. Then surely we can cajole that tired old iron horse into clunking on forward just as it always has. Yes! That has to be the solution doesn't it? Just go on believing what we always believed, go on doing what we always did and surely this too will pass. Until it doesn't. Until experience sits there slap bang on top of the guide rails, resolutely refusing to move and we can't go any further. What shall we do then?

What indeed?

14 Only The Mind Is Moving

There is an old Buddhist parable concerning two monks standing in a monastery garden. *Look,* says the first, pointing to a large, mature tree. *The tree is moving.* The second monk looks at the tree and considers it carefully. *No,* he replies. *The tree is not moving. It is the wind that is moving.* On and on they dispute, until the Abbott appears. *Which of us is right, Master?* they ask. *Is it the tree that is moving or is it the wind? Neither,* answers the Abbott. *The tree and the wind are both still. Only the mind is moving.*

I have had some sense of making progress in my personal development these last few weeks. Meditation Practice has been deep, sometimes with great insight, from which I return to day-to-day activities almost as if I am landing from a trip off-planet. Writing Practice, too, has flowed easily. Often, before I put pen to paper, the words begin to form. What a contrast this is to how it was for me just three years ago when I began meditating seriously, trying to flee an inescapable depression that seemed to rule my every waking hour. Now, it seems, calm and equanimity are my close friends. But sometimes those friends withdraw to teach me more by their absence than they can by their presence.

Sometimes sleep comes hard. I regularly rise early, normally between 5.00 and 6.00 in the morning, with the result that I am prone to falling asleep in the evenings. If I am not careful, this in turn makes it hard to get a good night's sleep. So I attempt to manage my hours of wakefulness and sleep carefully. I do not always achieve that. Last night I had successfully maintained my routine, switching off my electronic devices by 8:30 pm, reading and meditating through until 10.00 pm. Lights were out by 10.15 and I fell into a deep sleep. But only until 3.00 am, when I sprang wide-awake. For half an hour I applied all the techniques I know to go back to sleep – counting down slowly, relaxing the muscles in my body from my feet, then my legs and onward up my body, which often works. But to no avail. At 3:30 I got up, made a cup of ginger tea and sat in my deep leather swivel rocking chair in my study (the chair predates my present vegetarian lifestyle by a decade or more and I have no plans to part with it. Doing so would not bring back to life the animal that was stripped of its skin in its manufacture. Disposing of it would show neither compassion nor respect to the animal that lost its life for the sake of a chair).

I read the newspaper online, I read some devotional books, without achieving any sense of connection. All the while I grew more concerned and more irritable as I pursued that elusive, blessed sleep that seemed always to be running just ahead of me, just out of my grasp. I tried meditating again, setting the timer for 30 minutes. My mind raced, showing no willingness to settle. I found myself fixating on obscure fictitious problems that would likely never confront me. I grew cross with myself, all the while trying so hard to return to a position of non-identification with thought, only to slip back into that identification as each thought arose in my mind.

7.00 am arrived. My planned visit to the gym seemed unwise in such a tired state. Growing more distraught and irritated at the turn of events, I began to question whether all of my time meditating these last three years had been completely wasted. *All this is nonsense*, I concluded, *a complete waste of time. There's simply no point in going on meditating if life is going to be like this.* Irritably, I stood and made my way into the lounge, where I consumed coffee, granola and the TV morning news, which always seems jam-packed with woe and worry.

Finally, I rose from the couch and hit the shower – a great place to break state, I find. Under the stream of water I finally let go of my frustration, realising that it did not matter, that everything passes, everything changes, that what arises will also assuredly subside.

And then I saw it: my shift from self-congratulation for progress and spiritual insight that had so easily transformed into irritation and overreaction at the first hint of challenge. It was then that I realised the world was no different today when I was experiencing frustration from how it was yesterday when I was moved by insight. The tree did not move and nor did the wind. Only my mind was moving.

15 Natalie

All this year I have been reading the books of Natalie Goldberg. As I mentioned in the introduction to this book, I first came across her last year when she was a guest teacher at an online Zen retreat I attended, run by Henry Shukman. This septuagenarian lady started her talk by smoothing down her shoulder length grey hair. *Look!* she declared. *I now have a hairdo instead of a hair don't!* An unusual way of starting a dharma talk by an unusual Zen teacher. My attention was caught immediately, for her quip spoke of a life in which she had experienced the straightjacket of unnecessary rules and regulations – a straightjacket now, with the benefit of a lifetime's experience, cast off.

Natalie went on to talk about what she called monkey mind – our common tendency to jump without realising it from what we are concentrating upon to something totally unconnected and then to grasp at it or attach to that. We get lost in our identification with thought, only to shake ourselves awake later and realise yes, we've done it again. It is a constant issue for those of us who are new to serious meditation, for meditation itself is a process of breaking our identification with what we are thinking, as we realise, slowly, that we are not our thoughts. Then comes the question: if I am not my thoughts, those monkey jumps that change so often, then what am I? It is a question that humans have been asking through the whole of recorded history and for long before that.

Through her many books, Natalie came quickly to have a dramatic impact on my writing, my practice and my thought. I learned that in the last century she had written a million-copy best seller on the subject of writing – *Writing Down The Bones*. But when I tried to buy a copy it proved to be out of stock with every supplier I knew. How unusual is that in a digital age? Finally, I tracked down a second hand copy in the United States. By the end of the first chapter, I was hooked. Natalie Goldberg was my new teacher. I read slowly and thoughtfully, one short chapter at a time, before my Meditation Practice, two or perhaps three times a day. Before I finished the book I had ordered the next volume – *The True Secret Of Writing* – and went on to do the same with that one. Then I started her three-volume autobiography – though it should be said that pretty much all I have read of Ms Goldberg's works are semi-autobiographical.

But in all of this Natalie kept coming back to the source of her own learning – her Zen teacher, Katagiri Roshi. The preoccupation in her writing with this man expanded further and further, like an inflating balloon, until it became near obsessional. The story of how he had been called from Japan in 1963 to help with the Zenshuji Soto Zen Mission in Los Angeles, how he had gone on to establish a Zendo in the sub-zero temperatures of Minnesota, 5.00am meditations to start each day, the day-long, then week-long, then three or four week-long retreats that were comprised of sitting on a cushion facing the wall, punctuated with slow walking and silent meals. An unbroken commitment to practice that ran into years and decades. You wonder why anyone would willingly put themselves through such austerity. You wonder why, until you see it. And when you see it, you willingly commit to it, or to your own version of it, because that practice is what chips away at the layers of fiction we build up around us to live in a world that prefers superficial illusions to supporting the emergence of tangible reality – the sweet stuff revealed in the grind of day-to-day practicalities.

Natalie left Minnesota to live in a New Mexico adobe house built from vehicle tyres and mud. Here, she went on to establish retreats incorporating free Writing Practice into the Zen model. But the influence of Katageri Roshi in her life and work continued visibly. The eventual death of her beloved teacher changed her preoccupation. If anything, that inflated balloon continued to rise higher and higher until eventually, as all balloons do, it rose too high and popped. The pinprick that changed everything was the discovery that this profoundly influential teacher had been indulging in extramarital affairs with several of his female pupils. When the news reached her, Natalie, by her own report, was first incredulous and then devastated. So much so that she penned another volume disclosing the unpalatable truth and exploring her reaction to it.

As I read that book, *The Great Failure*[8], I felt her pain deeply. This teacher that she had eulogised and elevated so high had tumbled in her estimation, crashing upon the rocks of disappointment, smashing his own reputation and threatening the edifice she had built on the foundation of her belief in him. Do you identify with Natalie's disappointment? I certainly do. So many, many times over the years I too have over-elevated a revered teacher to a status where I confuse them with the teaching itself. For most of us that confusion usually ends, often with a painful crush of emotion and sometimes an overreaction of anger or disappointment. But the truth of the learning the teacher brought does not need to be lost. After that first flush of pain, if we are fortunate, we set aside the disappointment to integrate the learning and, most important of all, to move forward. I acknowledge and hail all my teachers who have brought me so much learning over so many years. I acknowledge them, and then release them. If I want to move on, it cannot be otherwise.

So, do us both a favour, if you will. When you have finished a book, any book, make a point of separating the author from any learning you have gained and move on to what comes next. Naturally, that includes me. I am full, so very full, of frailty and weakness. And I do not want you to suffer from confusing me with any illumination my books help you to gain.

Namaste. Be happy.

16 Elastic Banned

It seems a long time since my last Writing Practice. Time is elastic, is it not? It shortens when we want the moment to continue unchanged and stretches out endlessly when we want it to be different from how it is. Yet we know time is just a constant measure, ticking off the moments of our lives, constant whether we are here consciously or not.

I can represent a future in which I have ceased to exist, or the past before my existence began, but I can do so only in this moment. This moment can hold representations of what we call past and future only as present experiences. In this moment I can represent a world without me, but I cannot actually experience a world without me. Ask me to focus on those representations, ask me to drill down deeply into what they actually are, and I can find only the constituent parts of now – the photographs of experiences passed, the pictures I can draw mentally to represent moments that might yet come. But are all contained within the album that is now.

During meditation this morning I was overwhelmed with anger at a relatively minor mistreatment I had suffered some time back. I had had an expectation, an idea of how something should be and I was attached to that representation. A slight, a diminution in my sense of self-worth, initiated a response in me that resonated back to other representations I hold, both conscious and unconscious. I latched on to similar experiences and memories of the time when I was too small to do anything about it. Back then, my reaction had been anger – the screaming rage of a two-year-old to be internalised later as the inward-focused anger that was the depression of adult life, until it became a pattern – a gestalt, if you will. A repeated habit of many, many moments building into a complex sense of values that eventually became what I refer to as 'me'. All experienced in the eternal moment that is now, because there is only now. Time is a construct in this moment, the past and the future no more than a theoretical line laid out in consciousness. And the longer I choose to live by that line, the longer I remain attached to an illusion, a representation I call 'me,' the more I suffer.

There comes an end point to our suffering if we choose to let it be so. It occurs when we release our attachment to past and future, to the pleasant and unpleasant, and allow ourselves to experience what actually is now. If I do that, the myopic preoccupation within me melts into the vast consciousness that is universal. And when I see that, I smile and feel compassion for that me I allowed to suffer for so long. Why ever did I do that? Why ever was I preoccupied with the slight of another person's self-preoccupation?

Happiness, equanimity, is found in letting go of that attachment.

17 Yr Wyddfa

There is such sweetness in letting go – writing without thought, without planning, without control and without correction. For one such as I who has led a life of intensive control it is refreshment – like drinking from an ice-cold mountain stream on a hot day.

There was such a day. We had climbed Yr Wyddfa – Mount Snowden, if you prefer the English name. I must have been about 14 or 15 years old. We had ascended to the top of the mountain where, in those days, there was no café and no refreshment. There was a railway – it was built in 1894 – but we had eschewed it, preferring to walk up the mountain. The climb was not so hard on that early summer morning, the sun in those pre-globally warmed days, not so hot. But we had not planned our trip very carefully and had taken no refreshment with us. Our enthusiasm for reaching our goal was undiminished by our thirst. We resolved that we would simply have to make our way down, and seek out a café or similar to buy cold drinks. But we descended by a different route from the one we had taken on the way up and happened upon a Corrie, a large mountain lake of pure, clear water. As soon as we saw it we ran to the pebble shoreline, dropped to our knees and drank and drank and drank. Never had I tasted such water. Pure, clear and oh, so cold! Refreshment cold enough to slake the thirst of both body and soul. No doubt we would have come to it on the way up if we had ascended by that route. But coming to the summit by a different path, then discovering refreshment as we descended was joy unparalleled. The sun shone gently down on us, the breeze wafted, rippling the surface of the lake, breaking gentle waves onto the pebbles where we knelt. We bowed to the lake and the sun, oblivious to the spiritual gesture we were making, unaware of the countless numbers who had done the same before us, slaking thirst by day, revering the moon by night. And by our ignorant receiving of the universal gift, we honoured the provider, and we honoured our part in the universe. Without realisation, we acknowledged our dependence on the universe about us, receiving its gift, revering its power.

It could have gone so differently. A descent by a different path, a better planned trip with flasks and cups, a mistaken turn: by any of these alternatives we would have missed it all. It was my first lesson in symbiosis, in gratitude, in the bounty out there when we honour spirit, when we accept every turn in the road for what it is. Joy when there is joy, disappointment when there is disappointment. And all released when it is time for the moment to pass. No clinging, no resentment, no attachment.

I have not thought of that day in over 50 years. And today it returns to me because for twenty minutes, I heed the advice: do not control; do not think; do not correct. Simply be and let what is about you be. Herein lies the path to the light.

18 Sackcloth And Ashes

Forgive me, for I have sinned. No, I am not and have never been a Catholic. But I have only 10 minutes for Writing Practice this morning. The curtailed time is not a penance. It is because I have to go over to the doctor's surgery and grovel – and this because I have just missed my 9:40 am blood test. I feel particularly penitent for this error, given the parlous state of the NHS: *Don't you know there's a shortage of appointments? Don't you know we can't afford to waste them? Don't you know that NHS time is precious?* I don't know if the receptionist will actually say any of that but I will hear it anyway.

However, once I have stopped beating myself up for my mistake, I am left with an interesting question: why do I feel so strongly about missing an appointment? And it is not just this one. I hate the thought of inconveniencing other people. I have at least one friend who is almost always late. It is as if by design – unconsciously, if not consciously. She has told me (in confidence, so you won't tell anyone will you?) that she can be ready to leave the house on time but will deliberately procrastinate, knowing it is going to make her late. That is behaviour so alien to me that it might as well originate off-planet. I could never stand the stress of that way of being. I am perpetually early for everything. Flights and trains of course – they don't wait for you. But pretty much everything else as well.

The positive side of this is that I am usually unhurried, have plenty of time to be in the moment, often to meditate, when I arrive early. But when I ask myself what drives the habit, I have to say that it is fear – fear of causing offence, fear of causing disappointment, fear of being criticised. I am not certain where this springs from but I rather think it is rooted in the need to reach outside of myself for approval by others.

This self-examination takes me deep. What do I do with knowledge like that? I do not yet know. I need to think on it, bring it into the conscious moment. Perhaps I should make a point of not being early for a while to see what happens – to observe how I feel when I behave counter-intuitively. Perhaps I shall emulate my perpetually late friend to see how that feels. But not now. Now I must dash. It is time to enter the surgery on my knees calling out *Woe is me, Woe is me*. And for that I absolutely must not be late.

19 Who Are You?

This process is becoming comfortable now. It has acquired the status of a habit pattern. The fear of not being able to produce the desired result has melted away and there is just the doing, just the writing.

Normally, we don't give much thought to our habits, the repeated processes of daily life. We rarely think about how we translate an intention from thought into action. For a big project, maybe we adopt a plan. But for, say, getting up from the chair, we just decide to do it and, well, do it. But stare into the face of that single act for a moment: you check your watch (the act of so doing itself being a miracle of biological engineering). You decide it is time to go, and the next moment your brain sends the intention of getting up right through the nervous system, instructing the appropriate muscles to contract. You push back the chair, rise to a vertical position, and walk away.

It was not always so. There was a time before you learned how to walk. A time you didn't know what walking was. A time you didn't know what your body was or what it could do. It took you a while to figure out that there was a world outside of your own consciousness. Then you realised that the pink thing in front of you – maybe for convenience we could call it a hand – was under your control. You learned that if you told it to, it would reach for some brightly coloured object, maybe a red rattle that had caught your attention. You grasped the red rattle with the pink hand and drew it closer to you. You found joy and satisfaction in that act of control. *Hey! This is fun*, you thought, as you pulled the red rattle towards you, as you pushed away the green plastic brick.

From there you realised you had a body and you could tell it what to do. One slow realisation after the next came to your awareness, until it clicked that those legs sticking out in front of you – you could use them to lever yourself up and move around. Thus, the habit of standing and walking began. At first it was a challenge. You fell over a lot. But you got up again and pretty soon you were walking around the furniture. If you were one of the lucky ones, doing so brought you approval from mother, father, or some significant other. You did it in part for the approval and you also did it simply for the joy of doing it, until you came to identify with the body that was doing things for you and you came to believe you were your body that moved, you were your mind that figured out how to move. When all the while, behind it all, the consciousness that was the first you, that was there before the mind thought and before the body moved, the real you, looked on.

The thoughts came and went. The desires rose up and died down, sometimes satisfied sometimes not. If they were mostly satisfied, you generated feelings that you enjoyed and called them happiness. The world was a good place to be. But if your desires were mostly frustrated, it brought feelings you did not like. You called that 'sad' and, maybe later, 'depressed'. And all the while, the original you, the consciousness that was there before the mind formed intention and before the body fulfilled it, the consciousness, looked on.

There came the day when you began to realise that these bright red rattles and green plastic bricks, the praises that came your way for standing and walking and learning to spell and coming first in maths or winning the egg and spoon race, were not enough. But by then the pattern was formed. *If these pleasures don't satisfy*, you decided, *I'll head out and get some brighter red rattle like, maybe, a new dress or even a lot of new dresses. I'll get some bigger green plastic bricks like maybe a new 4x4, or more approval, a group of friends, a girlfriend, a boyfriend.* Anything to make you feel better.

The rattles and the bricks changed shape, became more complex as your thinking became more complex.

The approval became more subtle, or came from more people. You were on a stage singing, or on a platform, elevated to a position of prominence. And all the time you were feeding this thing called ego. And all the time, the original you, the consciousness that came before the mind, formed preferences, and the body did its best to deliver those cravings, your consciousness, the real you, looked on.

Here's a question for you. When do you get lucky? When do you take the time to start digging back deep into the self that you think you are to find the consciousness that lies behind the construct? Because it's still there, hiding in plain sight. If you can't see it, it's only a matter of focus. It's only because you have spent a lifetime looking at red rattles and green 4x4s, listening to the praises or deprecation heaped, checking your approval rating and the number of likes on your apps. And why would you look deeper than that? Why would you lay aside the rattles and the 4x4s and the power? Only because they're all coming to an end in their own good time anyway. Only because there's a reason the original you arrived in this body and mind in the first place. And you might want to get a little curious as to what that reason might be.

Today, maybe take a moment to release your focus on the next thought, the next deadline, the next purchase, the next date. Maybe let it all fade for just a moment or two and become aware of the consciousness that is the original you. Because if you do, you may just start to discover how enormous and how wonderful the real original you actually is. Because that's when the rattles and the 4x4s start to pale in the sunlight of awareness and the need for approval melts like snow in the sunshine and the warmth of self-awareness that is love.

20 Matt And Me

Matt, my hearing dog, is on my mind this morning. He died four years ago yesterday. I had a note in my diary to remind me but I somehow managed to miss it, even though he was the sun and the moon and the stars, my light and my joy, the focus of my writing and my life for more than 15 years. Before he arrived, I would never have conceived it possible to experience this close a relationship with an animal. But beyond being my joy, he was my hearing, my lifeline into a hearing world.

When Matt passed, I was offered a successor hearing dog. I considered the offer for a year before declining. There were several reasons for doing so, not least of which is that I now have a cochlear implant and many other people need these dogs more than I do. But I guess the most important reason was that I knew nothing could ever come close to being able to replace him. A part of me died with him and I have spent much of the intervening period grieving for him.

It's not like that now though. I think back on him with joy and warmth beyond measure. He still makes me laugh when he comes to mind – those games of mock aggression when I adopted a defensive posture and growled at him. He would leap at me in feigned attack, latching onto my arm with a grip that managed to be both immovable and gentle at the same time. Then I would collapse onto the floor in laughter and he would smother me with licks as I cried out over and over, *No more doggy kisses! We don't need any more doggy kisses.* He did his damnedest to get his tongue in my mouth and I didn't always manage to stop him. How can anything be vile and disgusting and hilarious at the same time?

I visited the site of his sprinkled ashes in Godshill Wood earlier this year. When I was about half a mile away, I felt his presence around me, a sense of joy, and adoration, of delight that I had come to see him again. He walked with me for upwards of half an hour, darting in and out of my awareness, just as he used to dart in and out of sight, disappearing into the dark undergrowth off the path so that I could not see him. He would crash around, terrorising every small creature within reach until I was convinced I had lost him forever. Then he would reappear on the path fifty metres ahead and look at me as if to say *What are you waiting for?* So we walked together that day for half an hour or so – an incarnate man and a disincarnate dog, the lack of body proving no impediment at all to his ability to convey joy, happiness and an irrepressible zest for life itself.

There may yet be another dog for me. I have considered adopting a rescue dog, where the purpose of doing so would be to give a home, more than to gain something back. But not yet. Not while I'm still out and about with book events fifty or sixty days a year, plus preparation time. And not while Matt is still monarch of my heart.

So why did I forget his anniversary yesterday? I guess it's simply a sign that I'm moving on. At no other time over the last four years could I have conceived that possible. The world turns on. Our days pass. We move into and out of one another's lives, in body, out of body. All is, as the Buddhists put it, Samsara. All is illusion. All is temporary. If we are wise, we hold all we have with the gentlest of grasps, just as his gentle jaws locked around my arm. We release that grip when it is time to let go. Attachment to desire is the cause of our suffering. So I release Matt in as much joy as I held him. Little by little, I let him slip away and do not hold him beyond the measure of his days.

21 The Loyal Toast

This Saturday, 7 May 2023, is the day of the coronation of the new King. We have been aware of the date for several months, watching as the news discloses increasing details of the extra bank holiday, the street parties, the Big Help Out, aimed at stimulating more people to devote their time to helping others. Of this I approve unreservedly.

But I must ask myself if I have not also sensed growing signs of attempted manipulation – the driving of a preferred narrative by those who speak, or purport to speak, for the monarchy. I am thinking of the apparent reluctance to facilitate reconciliation between the King and his second son; a progressive agenda to normalise the uneasy role of His Majesty's second wife, first referred to as Queen Consort and now Queen, reportedly on the instructions of the late Queen; daily press releases, videos and pictures showing how the nation has apparently taken her to heart. I also note the absence of rail strikes for this weekend in contrast to a clear strategy by rail union organisers to inconvenience travellers to many other national events on many other weekends both before and after this one.

Perhaps it would be uncharitable to suggest that if you speak a hope as if it were a truth for long enough, it first becomes a belief and eventually, if you persist in controlling the narrative, an accepted fact. Regrettably, this also requires the airbrushing of history to remove uncomfortable references to His Majesty's first wife, once so beloved of the nation and now evolved into 'she-who-must-not-be-named'.

I have genuine sympathy with those whose job it is to promote the institution of royalty in 2023. The lately deceased Queen was an impossibly hard act to follow, beloved as she was by billions across the world. An icon of an age now over, the name and figurehead by which an era will be written into history. Her passing marks a watershed. Many who esteemed her and tolerated, for her sake, an institution they otherwise considered to be an anachronism, appear disinclined to sustain their forbearance into a third Carolean age.

For my part, I esteem the new holder of the crown at a personal level. He espoused the cause of planetary conservation and, reportedly, even the hugging of trees, long before it became fashionable to do so. He also declared, decades ago, that he would eschew the title 'Defender of The Faith' in the favour of being known as 'Defender of Faiths'. As far as we distant masses can judge, this is a monarch who has the vision and capacity to work for good in the world. Please God (or should that be gods?) that he will rise sufficiently to the role to see through the machinations of the manipulators, the schemers and rewriters of history.

This morning, I looked at a news item concerning our new Queen and felt a deep compassion come upon me. Whatever the wrongs and foolishness of the past, today we are where we are. Here I see an individual who is doing her best to work for good in the world and to be accepted. I look back upon my personal history and wince at some of the ill-advised and selfish decisions I took in the past. I acknowledge that, however unwise my younger behaviour, each decision, each step I have taken along the way, has brought me to now and, I hope and trust, to a little more awareness, illumination and compassion than I knew in years gone by. Our Royal Family are primarily human beings, however far elevated above us their entourages would like them to appear. Perhaps we should express a deeper compassion for those of a generation and social class for whom an emotionally deprived upbringing was a normal expectation.

On Saturday, I shall not be swearing allegiance to their majesties, for I shall be otherwise occupied. But I wish them, as I wish all sentient beings, happiness and freedom from suffering. Today I raise my loyal toast to King Charles III, butter it and eat it in his name, as I declare the only advice I would presume to offer for his auspicious day:

King, save the gods.

Love light and peace to you both.

22 Switching Off The Treadmill

Today is busy. I started with normal meditation and readings at 5.30am, was at the gym shortly after 7.00, and then came to Costa café for early Writing Practice. Later this morning there will be an author interview on Zoom. A book delivery is due this afternoon. But at this moment all of that is shrieking *STOP!* at me very loudly.

I find it all too easy to become reabsorbed back into the merry-go-round, the dash of life that, if we are not careful, channels us from event to event, deadline to deadline, target to target, until sometime between seventy and eighty years of age, for most of us, it all just stops. Then you wonder why you did it, why you deemed it all so important. There are the fundamentals of feeding yourself and your family, certainly, the providing of accommodation, the doing of your best for your children. It all makes perfect sense and I don't mean to criticise it. But if we pursue it all for its own sake, we get lost in the activity. The treadmill becomes a mindless stomping, pace after pace, event after event. And just like when I'm on that treadmill at the gym, we forget that the sense of forward movement is illusory, that when we turn off the machine, we discover that we have travelled nowhere.

Yesterday, my brother sent me a family tree he had been researching of our lineage. Back through the decades of East London Jewish life it stretched, one generation begetting another; birthing, growing, conjoining, breeding, ageing, expiring. Life after life, generation after generation, all of us doing essentially the same thing. And most of us, most of the time, giving little thought to why we do it. At the end of that long lineage, here am I. Starting my day with meditation, then running from one appointment, one deadline to the next, focused so deeply on the preoccupation that I forget that I am living in one infinitesimally small heartbeat of history.

So I'm glad of the opportunity to stop and remind myself of that. That same awareness of the moment which I allowed to absorb me in meditation, that expansion of awareness to the whole – that is the centeredness of spirit with which I want to hold my day. Mindfulness is not just sitting, not just writing. It is standing in line for coffee and connecting to the people who serve me. It is driving home on roads where others like me are focused on their moment, barely aware that we are interacting. It is opening my heart in a Zoom interview to let viewers see as much of who I am as I am capable of showing them. It is appreciating that the driver who delivers my books is a whole person with a home, problems and people he or she cares about. All are trying to do a decent job as each perceives it to be, or maybe just pushing through a task they have lost connection with. I interact with them for the briefest of moments then we go our separate ways, back to all the challenges and pleasures of our respective lives. We are all whole people, bringing the entirety of ourselves to an interaction. But we are each apt to see only what appears before us, the presentation in the flash of a moment. We easily ignore what is not obviously disclosed, what emerges in the silence that descends when the day's activities are done.

May I, this day, be in awareness of each moment, knowing that spirit, that dancing emptiness, that lies behind it all. And in so doing, may I remember that all of the activity is merely Samsara – illusory, transient. In that awareness, may I release ego, connect with Big Mind and be kind to all whom I encounter today.

23 In A Moment

I am staying in Dorset, looking out over an ocean that is changing colour before my eyes. A 24-hour storm has blown itself out and the sky is turning from grey to a more congenial china blue, dotted with the puffy white clouds that trademark an English summer. Years ago, storms of this nature were unremarkable at this time of year. We experienced changeable weather for which the UK is famous and discussed its instability from day to day. As a nation, we became as well-known for our propensity to talk about the weather, as our weather was known for its unreliability. But recently, global warming has apparently changed all that. Each summer has tended to be long and hot, peaking at previously inconceivable temperatures, leaving the grounds and plants gasping and withering. If you don't get your fuel you cannot bloom as you were intended to do.

As our summers have become hotter and more stable, fewer Brits have been inclined to take summer holidays abroad. A combination of pandemic, followed by Brexit inconvenience and air traffic control strikes has increasingly disinclined us to venture beyond our borders. So, more of us have looked for holiday accommodation in the UK and the price of AirBnB accommodation has soared accordingly. Then, literally out of the blue, came yesterday's storm. It arrived as I pulled up in the car in the morning and grew in intensity throughout the day, its grey skies dumping a seemingly an ending torrent over an angry, greyer sea.

What satisfied the thirst of the fields and gardens has decimated the plans of many. We premeditate our actions on the expectations of consistency. We form an outcome, an aim, based on the belief that the world about us is reasonably predictable. We devote our budgets, commit our time and then cross our fingers. Sometimes all occurs in accordance with our hopes. We are blessed with sunshine; the children and the dogs play happily on the beach as a gentle sea laps waves onto the shore. But how often is this not so? How often are our plans brought to nothing by a change in circumstances? The storm that blows up unexpectedly. The train that is late. The health diagnosis that reveals all is not well. Then there is pain. We suffer in proportion to how attached we were to our hoped-for outcome. I was hoping for a day on the beach.

He was hoping to get to that crucial meeting in town to secure a deal. She was hoping for ten more years of life, at least. Then we realise all is not going to be as we had planned. Our representation of happiness or satisfaction that depends on the external is revealed as just that – not a reality, but just a representation. Some expectations are easy to release, others much less so. We shrug our shoulders at the weather and determine to holiday somewhere more reliable next year. We become angry at the loss of the expected: the business deal that was never more than a hope set in an arrogant determination to bend the world to our will; the belief that life itself owes us more years yet. We consider we have not received what we are entitled to. With expectations dashed and promise curtailed, we fall to grieving what never was.

In this moment we can carry memory of the past, accurate or otherwise, and we can conjure a representation of the future, pleasant or unpleasant. But both are nothing more than energy patterns in my mind at this moment. Ultimately, we have only this moment. The past, if it ever was as we represented it, with its apparent joys and sadness, is not here in this moment. The future may or may not turn out to be as we are mapping it.

We mark our existence moment by moment. Our experience of happiness or suffering is determined by our willingness or unwillingness to let the moment pass. Today, may I choose to hold my reality upon an open palm, offering no resistance when it flies away, as it surely must. I know what I want and enjoy it as it occurs. But I release it when its time is done, accepting that the next moment may or may not be as pleasing to me. But whatever that forthcoming moment offers, it too will pass. And in my willingness to let it do so without clinging to it lies my equanimity.

24 Sounds And Silence

In Costa café today, the ice crusher is in great demand and the hubbub of conversation is rising high, as people try to be heard above it. If I were meditating formally, I would leave my implant in place and simply slide down through the layers of sound, gradually becoming aware of the silence from which all thoughts and everything material arises. But today, whilst writing, I prefer to start with silence, so I have removed my cochlear implant hearing processor.

I had not heard properly for some 30 years or more when this device was fitted. Over the decades my natural hearing had declined and eventually, to all practical purposes, disappeared. After the operation, I spent a month in total silence, waiting for the wound to heal before the external component could be attached.

Think about that for a moment. Total silence. No sound

at all for a month. I travelled out and about, but spoke to almost no one. And when I did, I could not hear their response. I was embarrassed enough to want the ground to open its jaws and let me sink down into invisibility. I did my best with lip-reading but without the support of a hearing aid it was never enough to achieve understanding. I spent my days posting poems on Facebook, texting, watching silent TV with subtitles, which, for live programs such as the news, are always a sentence or two behind the voice of the speaker. And then, a month later, the external part of the device was fitted.

The world instantly filled with noise. But all I heard was an electronic hiss of meaningless squeaks and rumbles. It would take another four weeks before I had re-learned how to hear sufficiently to distinguish speech, and then at first everyone sounded like the Supreme Dalek – voice distinction took longer to achieve. Ironically, the first voice I heard properly instructed me to *take the next turning on the right*. I had never heard the satnav before.

But a couple of weeks after that, I was booked on a flight to Bangkok and from there on another to Kathmandu, making a pilgrimage in search of the singing bowls of the Himalayas, taking the next step on my journey, seeking contact with those who knew spirit in a way I did not. And I found it all. If you want to know more about that trip, take a look at my travelogue, *One Journey,* which documents its ups and downs (spiritual as well as physical), its challenges and joys.

Now, seven years have passed. In the meantime I have sometimes forgotten that I am a deaf person living in a hearing world – until a battery fails and there is silence or until one of my frequent mishearing experiences leads me to make an inappropriate response with hilarious or painful results – quite often both. I am a deaf man. I no longer feel any shame or embarrassment for so being. I adjust to the best of my ability and sometimes others around me are kind enough to adjust too, so that together we reach across the divide to join soul-to-soul. I seek no sympathy. There is an undercurrent, a pervading joy to being who I am for as long as I am in this body, in this lifetime. And there is a deeper joy in digging down through the sound into the layers of silence to feel the consciousness, the emptiness that lies all around everything, from which everything that has form emerges. Some call that God and if you do, I salute you. But you don't need silence to encounter that space, that person, if you will. All you need to do is stop, release your focus on the illusion of the material world and the preoccupation before you and allow the emptiness to come to you.

And that is enough for today. I shall reattach my processor now, make eye contact with the first person that is open to doing so, smile and connect if I can. And for the floodgates of love to open in so doing, I need no hearing.

25 Showtime

The opportunity for learning is all about you when you open your eyes – in your own behaviour, and in the behaviour of others. If you are willing to be present in the moment and break your identification with thought, then it is there for the taking, for the learning.

For the last three days, I have been signing books for readers at the New Forest Show, my single most important sales event of the year. Although it is repeatedly successful for me in terms of numbers of books purchased, it can also be a cause of stress. That stress, as is almost always the case with stress, is self-imposed. No one makes me attend the event. No one set targets for me. But I excel at setting targets for myself and expend much energy on the pursuit of them once set. Stress invariably arises when I want something, when I want to change the way the moment is.

So I sit at the show, waiting for visitors to drop by and chat to me at my table, and I show them my books. Often these lovely folk do buy the books for themselves, or as gifts. But if a period of time passes without that happening, I can grow irritated, concerned that I will miss my self-imposed target on which nothing at all depends – nothing except my pride, that is. No one will stand at the exit as I drive away jeering at me for my failure if I undershoot my target. No one will applaud my success if I achieve target. All my stress depends on my own estimation of what I should be achieving and how.

While all this is going on for me, show visitors come and go, absorbed in their own concerns, the stresses, pressures and joys of their own lives. There are those whose connections are straightforward. Their smiles are honest, whether they say yes or no to the offer of a book. There are those whose faces light up when they see a cover they connect with – dogs, dragons, forests, or whatever it happens to be.

Then there are those who have a clearly-defined agenda, which is a little more covert – the woman who approaches to tell me about Jesus, for example. She spies the subtitle of my book *Vicious*, that reads 'A novel of punk rock and the second coming.' She takes offence that I have hijacked the words 'second coming' for the mere cover of a frivolous book – all without so much as picking up a copy and turning it over, or dipping into the pages, you understand. I am granted the benefit of her declaration of how wonderful it is to be a Christian. I bow to her and thank her for sharing her thoughts with me. As she walks away, I find myself wondering whether her affirmations concerning her Saviour are for my benefit or whether they are more about her need for reassurance that the path that she has chosen in life is the 'right' one. I will likely never get to meet her again to find out. Then, there is the very elderly lady who criticises my prices. They don't seem high to me in comparison with other books, but she expects more for less. Quite often I give books away when there is a need (I did so several times at this event, as it happens). But in this case, I refrain, sensing her reprimand as arising less from being unable to afford a book and more from the need to externalise her pain. I do not criticise. I know nothing of her journey, her aspirations and hopes, whether realised or dashed.

I watch parents buy *Dragonsong*, an epic fantasy poem in ancient rhyming verse, for little boys too young to read the sophisticated poetry. I wonder whether the book is purchased for the child or more to satisfy the parents' aspirations for the child – vicarious living in the making. I watch the careful planners, buying six discounted books at a time in July to put away as Christmas presents. I watch the young couple that return just as I am packing away at the end of the last day of the show. They bought three books from me earlier, but now realise they also wanted my dystopian volume, *A Home For Other Gods*. I take a copy from the box, dedicate it to Tana and smile as they walk away, happy.

Then I load up the car with the tables and the roller banners, the carrier bags and the boxes of books. And I drive away having sold 195 books against a hoped-for figure of 200. Am I sad at the shortfall? Am I less fulfilled than if I had sold 205, or 405, or 4500 on Amazon? Not at all. It is as it is. I cannot change this moment and I have stopped wanting it to be different from how it is, for therein lies the highway to suffering. I remind myself of what I have written in *Forest Pathways*: when I learn to accept everything, I can change anything.

I have touched lives this week in ways I will never know – for good, I hope, in every case. I am still a learner and in this lifetime always will be. I still need to make a conscious practice of breaking my identification with my thoughts, of emerging from the darkness of self-judgement into the light of compassionate awareness. Today, I am glad of The New Forest Show and my days spent there. Little by little, I am chipping away at my attachment. Little by little, I am opening to the light.

26 The Family Way

Yesterday, I hosted a family summer party for eleven people – modest enough by most people's standards but quite a challenge if you are deaf. Hearing difficulty, even with a cochlear implant, rises exponentially with the number of people in the room and geometrically with a number of people trying to talk at the same time.

It was a wet and overcast day, with rain tumbling indiscriminately over the garden and the sun thinking better of putting in an appearance. A severe storm had decimated the display of flowers in the planter outside the window the previous week, denuding the geraniums of their delicate red and pink petals. Only the deep violet of the delphiniums behind them still stood proud, their colour shining like beacons through the dark grey drizzle. We, like the bees, are designed to be drawn to colour, to eschew shades of grey, letting our eyes delight more readily in what is bright and attractive to us. Of course, grey comes in mental and spiritual shades as well as physical.

And so it was with the conversations of those of us sitting inside, protected from the ravages of weather as the plants and insects cannot be. I stood back from the hubbub of indistinguishable (well, to me, anyway) conversations, as uncles and nieces reacquainted themselves after a year of absence, and cousins of dramatically varying ages politely enquired as to one another's state of health, or education, or gainful employment. All very normal family stuff, the challenges of different people, of different mindsets, some a little less tactful or a little more sensitive than others would prefer, some who find it hard to relate for reasons we might explore another day. All differences were set aside for a few hours of buffet and congeniality. Grey hair and balding heads juxtaposed blonde teenage manes, worlds collided, lit up in the brilliance of a smile, as common ground was found in a vast sea of difference. No one went away unhappy or sorry they had come. No one became overtly angry or apparently took offence. No one vowed never to speak to somebody else ever again. All found something to value in the others, even though as individuals we could not be more different.

And when they had all left and my house returned to its habitual state of silence, the peace that pervaded the atmosphere seeped through me. A challenging day, I reflected, but a thoroughly worthwhile one nevertheless and one I aim to repeat next year. It's called family. It's called love.

27 White Rabbits

Today is 1st August and on this new month I start a new page. Open spaces can offer the chance to start again, a sense of possibility, of excitement and opportunity. We feel the same thing on a greater scale when the turn of the year arrives. Indeed, if you go back further to when the millennium turned, the sense of new possibility was enormous, close to overwhelming. Here is a chance to do things differently, we thought, to get it right, to make it better, to cast off what we do not want. But for most of us, the feeling did not last long.

When you think about it, every calendar change, every turn of every page is nothing more than a human construct; a delineation of convenience, a subdivision of the biggest human construct of all: time itself. So why do we see it this way? Why is there a sense of excitement as we turn a page on the calendar or dance our way into a new year? Perhaps it is because of the way we think about this thing called time itself, our methodology of subdividing the heartbeats of our lives into groups that our minds find convenient. Perhaps we want to put into the past all that we have done that we regret or that we wish we had done differently. We want to turn a page on it, turn our back on it, create a state of mind whereby we allow ourselves to do it differently.

But when I delve deeper into my own thinking, I have to own that every moment is unique. The turning of a number on the calendar is no different from the steady beat of my heart, the pumping of each measure of blood, the inhalation of each breath. The truth is that every moment is a new opportunity, entirely distinct from the last, influenced by the past only to the extent that I allow it to be, constrained as to the future only by the beliefs I choose to carry forward with me on my journey.

There is no need to wait for a new day, a new month or a new year to do something differently. This moment is the only moment we really have. And in this moment we can choose to be. To be what you ask? A writer? An accountant? A carpenter? All of these and none of them. As for me, my choice and focus in the moment is simply to be – to celebrate my own amazing existence – and yours too. In this moment I celebrate your uniqueness and mine, our connection and commonality, the diversity and integration of being. This is the moment of now and it is a good moment to be filled with the amazement and joy of everything that is.

28 Chewing Old Lettuce

Sometimes I find myself thinking about writing these Flashes in advance. I visualise myself sitting down, selecting a subject, then writing. I come up with lots of good ideas that way. But I always dispense with them. If I try to use them it's like chewing week-old lettuce. You have to pick salad vegetables and eat them as quickly as possible. They're never quite the same if you come back to them later. And so these ideas I visualise disappear back into the emptiness. When I sit before the page, I choose a new subject that bubbles up as I take my pen in hand, then press on to see where it takes me. But what of those ideas that take form in my mind which I release and never use? What happens when they dematerialise? Indeed, what happens to all thought when it evaporates? For that is what all thoughts do, of course.

What were you thinking about just before you picked

up this text and began reading? If you can remember at all, you are likely at best to have a vague impression of it, a kind of lingering shadow-thought of your first thought. And yet we place such value on these transient coagulations that constitute our ideas and beliefs: that the world is round or flat, that fossil fuels are harmful to the planet or not, that to spare the rod is to spoil the child, or not. All outmoded ideas were once held in earnest, gripped in an iron fist so firmly that their proponents would do anything in defence of their beliefs, even to the point of terminating the lives of others who disagreed or failed to conform. The decapitator crying Allah Akbar is the child of the Spanish inquisitor and first cousin to the Aryan ethnic cleanser.

All those deeply held beliefs, obnoxiously wrong and outmoded to the modern mind. We know better than preceding generations, do we not? We persist in our dearly-held beliefs, certain that those other beliefs cherished in the past were wrong and that what we hold to with such determination now, that is the truth, that is the right way of doing things, that is what is universally best – and anyone who disagrees be damned. We hold up the traffic with slow marches. We storm Congress. We fire missiles indiscriminately into container ships to draw attention to what we believe to be injustice. We deny women the right to work or to visit the beautician. All beliefs. All deeply cherished by their proponents. All vehemently resisted by their opponents. Ideas, rising and falling with the moment, with the turning of the world, with the turning of the year, with the turning of one lifetime, many lifetimes. Each yielding to the next generation, who will believe just as vehemently that we, their predecessors, were wrong and should have known we were wrong.

Sobering, isn't it? That however deeply you cherish a belief, it will pass. Its time will pass. It will become regarded as at best outmoded, or quaint, or at worst, downright despicable. Hold onto your ideas and beliefs loosely today. For when their time comes they will spread their wings and fly away, whether you want them to or not. Hold just to this: love.

29 Where Oak Trees Bow

I write today of our responses to the unplanned, since I am sitting here unexpectedly. The first day of an event I was due to attend – the New Forest Food and Craft Festival – has been cancelled.

I should make it clear that it is fairly common for me to experience cancellation of a few outdoor engagements each year due to the unpredictability of the British weather. And this year is no exception. We were doing quite well, with no cancellations right up until the end of July. We had planned the August schedule based on last year, with more concern for the possibility of another 40° heat wave than with any thought of rain or storm. But July's record rainfall has filled the reservoirs to overflowing, smoothing the furrowed brows of stressed water company executives up and down the land. Hosepipe bans seem highly unlikely this year. But now, with the coming of August, arrives storm Antoni, our third named summer storm and the first one this year.

Yesterday, I knew severe weather was on its way but chose to set up for the event anyway, living in hope that it would not be too bad. I erected my gazebo, taking care not to raise it to its full height, then set up my tables and covered everything with plastic sheets. Having weighed it all down diligently, I drove home and spent a quiet evening waiting to see what would happen. When I woke this morning, there had been just a little rain. But within minutes, my friend and helper Sue, who lives sixty miles west of me, messaged to warn me of high winds and lashing rain. The West Country often gets the weather system a couple of hours before we do here in the New Forest. I might have started to worry at that point. I might have begun to visualise catastrophe, with tent and tables and books strewn across the field, and desperate people chasing after their possessions through near zero visibility. But I did not.

Instead, I went to the gym as normal, and then drove the few miles to the show in order to arrive at my planned time. As I set off, the wind picked up and the rain intensified, blowing near horizontally on the road where I live. I watched the great oak trees in the copse behind my house swaying and bowing, as great oaks will, paying fealty in leaves to the angry storm. Antoni clearly does not like to be underestimated.

When I arrived at the show ground, my gazebo was still erect, though a bit buffeted and blown. But within half an hour the organisers had cancelled the day's activities. So I made sure everything was as secure as possible, zipped the tent back up and drove my faithful Skoda Octavia out over a waterlogged field, relieved I did not get stuck in the rapidly increasing amount of mud. The event was planned to last two days. We hope to open tomorrow.

Now I sit once more in the café. The rain has already stopped. My gazebo may have blown down in the last of the storm, of course. But I have no way of knowing here, sipping coffee in the warm. Nevertheless, I shall not return to check until tomorrow. It will be as it will be. I cannot change anything about that in this moment. I hope to return to find an undamaged gazebo and contents and go on to enjoy a clement day, meeting readers and signing books for them, as I love to do.

But I hold that hope upon an open palm, knowing full well that the day will eventually come that will be my last day of meeting readers and signing books. And from my palm, that activity will fly away. I don't think it will happen tomorrow. But I could be wrong. And if it is, well, that is simply the nature of transience, in a universe that is always changing. I love it but I do not attach to it, I do not grip it.

So today I pray that will be my mode of behaviour for

all that I love and all that I value.

Namaste.

May you, and I, and all beings be happy.

30 Glorious Mud

I was a bit premature with yesterday's Flash when I expressed hope that we might be able to proceed with the New Forest Food and Craft Festival today. For, last night at 9:30, I received an email from the organisers to tell me that the second day of the show had also been cancelled. I penned a response of sadness – more for them than for me, it being their first ever event, and confirmed my intention to join them again next year. Then I headed off to bed and read before falling asleep. The next morning, today, I was up ultra early at 3.00 am. That sometimes happens to me, I wake in the night and can't go back to sleep. So I undertook an early meditation and read further in my devotional books. The most pertinent passage spoke of how we create most, if not all of, our own suffering by our unwillingness to accept the moment as it is.

Then, just before 8:30 am, I set off for the showground.

Wisely, the organisers had opened a new gate where the ground was a little less rutted with deep tyre marks and I was able to drive straight onto the field which was, it has to be said, a quagmire. Nevertheless, via a few skids and slithers, I arrived relatively easily enough at my gazebo. I packed away everything I had brought plus a little mud and got back in the car. It was then I saw that a car belonging to another trader, a young woman, was stuck in the mud near the entrance. I went to help and also to scope out whether there was another way for me to get past her car without getting stuck in the increasing number of ruts in the ground near the exit. There wasn't. So four of us pushed her car and she managed to get away, both her and the vehicle liberally splattered with mud. I, by contrast, was relatively mud free. I counted my blessings.

I returned to my car and thought I would try doing the same. I aimed at the gate, picked up speed nicely and thought I was going to make it, until I too got stuck in a rut. A burly gentleman with a large tractor approached, checked under the car and saw that I had a mount for a tow bar at the back. *Where's the tow bar?* he asked. I looked whimsically at him and pointed to the car. *It's underneath everything I've just packed away,* I said sadly. *Can you give me a push instead of a tow please?*

Not looking best pleased, he called over to a couple of colleagues and together they pushed me backwards onto the virgin grass. Then he indicated an exit at the opposite end of the field and told me to have a try at going through there. The problem was that I hadn't really understood where he meant. Deafness is like that. *Go between those two vehicles,* he said, waving vaguely south. Unfortunately there were quite a few vehicles to choose from and I chose the wrong ones. I then drove to the far end of the field where I promptly found myself stuck in the mud again.

It was then I began to become irritated. *This is ridiculous,* I said under my breath. *I helped someone else so why won't they help me? I'm not coming back here again next year!* And then I recognised that what I was feeling was anger. And I knew that I was creating my own suffering by failing to accept the moment as it was.

Of course, I had a solution all along: the tow bar. It was just that I didn't want to go to the trouble of unpacking the car again to get it. So I acknowledged where equanimity lay and unpacked boxes and tables and gazebo onto my tarpaulins. I retrieved said tow bar from the spare tyre underneath it all, feeling rather pleased with myself, for I had learned an important lesson. Never mind that I was now covered in mud. I was making spiritual progress.

By this time, the burly gentleman was approaching. I held up the tow bar smiling. He examined it closely. He pushed it and pulled it and twisted it and turned it. And then he looked at me and said, *Sorry, I don't know how this attaches. We'll have to push you!* All my effort was wasted. I knew immediately that what I was feeling was frustration.

It was then that I learned a second lesson in accepting the moment as it was.

Three muscular gentlemen then proceeded to push my vehicle off the field into the lane where I did not stop, lest I became stuck again. Battle weary and liberally coated in mud (that's much of my stock, all of my car and most of me), I am now home. It is my intention to go back to this show next year. I have sold no books at all but I have learned an enormous amount about where peace lies, and it isn't in getting what I want exactly when I want it.

31 The Stars Wait For No One

Well it's Costa, Jim, but not as we know it.

I have migrated today from wet and dreary New Milton, which was looking decidedly soggy after overnight rain, to the sunnier climes of Southampton General Hospital. Well, of course, it's not even a little bit sunnier than New Milton, being a mere 37 minutes drive away, according to Google Maps. Grey streets and grey skies have given way to more grey streets and equally grey skies. What was I saying a month or two ago about summer weather having become hotter in the UK? Well forget it. Climate change may be bringing life-claiming fires to some places, such as poor Maui, but here in the UK we seem to get more of the same: unpredictable cloudbursts interspersed with the merest glimpse of the sun when it registers its presence every third Tuesday or so. Climatically, life is looking decidedly normal.

So what am I doing in the hospital? I make my own share of visits here, which I guess is typical at the grand old age of 68. But today I have dropped Jacqui off for a consultation of her own and made my usual beeline to my favourite coffee outlet. I ordered my habitual coffee in the reusable plastic cup (courtesy of a visit to the Hay on Wye book Festival in 2017 where, sadly, I was neither speaking nor reading) with brown toast and four pats of butter. In New Milton, I take my seat and a kindly and invariably young barista brings my toast and butter on a white plate, placed daintily on a tray, together with steel knife and serviette. But on Planet Southampton Hospital they do things differently. I wait while my order is prepared, then I am presented with it. Coffee is in the reusable cup as normal for sure, but the toast and butter arrive in a little white paper bag. I am directed to a stand, where I can collect a balsawood knife and encouragingly unbleached serviette. Then I make my way to an empty table, where I use the paper bag as a plate. I have extracted the butter not a moment too soon, for placed next to the toast in the bag, it is on the point of turning into a lake of something molten and yellowish, that somehow puts me in mind of erupting volcanoes and the formation of planet Earth.

My mind wanders back to childhood, when my Welsh grandparents travelled from the Neath Valley to visit us in our North London suburban home. Amongst other outings, they took my brother and me for a walk on

Hampstead Heath and thence to a little coffee house about a hundred yards (not metres you understand – this was the 1960s) away, where we each chose a drink and a cake. Four drinks and four cakes served on plates – yes, real plates – with white linen napkins and China teacups. And for this delectable little afternoon repast we were charged ten shillings. Yes, ten whole shillings! My grandfather was astounded at the eye-wateringly price. If you remember old money, you'll know that ten shillings became 50p – half of £1.00. Try getting tea and cake times four for that now in Neath, never mind Hampstead, and they would double up in laughter. The value of money has changed.

So have expected standards. Or at least commonly available standards have, which is why I am eating my toast from a paper bag today. Had we been eating toast and coffee that day in the Hampstead of the 1960s, it would have tasted much the same then as it does now. But gone are my expectations of fabric serviettes, china plates and similar gentility. Somewhere in between then and now, a few thousand per cent of inflation landed. As the human population doubled and the planet warmed, the approval rating of gasoline-fuelled cars and coal-heated homes plummeted. We live differently now because we have to. We drop the expectations of our grandparents together with our own habits of a lifetime because if we do not, the grandchildren of our grandchildren will not have a lifetime.

Yesterday, at the New Forest Fairy Festival, I dedicated a book to a gentleman who told me his name was Elishium-Dai. It translates, he told me, as 'the stars wait for no one.' I have to acknowledge the truth of the sentiment. The world has turned so very many times since my grandfather's day. The stars might look the same from the distance at which we observe them, but they have travelled inestimable distances since the 1960s. And so have we. Our world is not what it was and our habits can no longer be as they were.

But our values don't have to change, though we might embody them differently. My grandfather wrapped his love for us in four drinks and cakes served on china crockery with napkins that day. Now I sit and write in the foyer of Southampton hospital, drink from a reusable cup and eating toast from a flattened paper bag, wondering how the world will look four generations hence. I hope that it will still be as beautiful a world for them to enjoy as the one my grandfather aspired for me to inhabit. I hope for it, but I am not certain, which is why I do everything I can to minimise my carbon footprint, from installing solar panels on my roof, to eating a vegetarian diet. The world cannot wait any longer for us to change our habits at the genteel pace of teahouses and napkins. The stars wait for no one and they will certainly not wait for me.

32 Letting Go

Write without thinking or correction, say the rules of Writing Practice, and without letting the hand stop for the allotted period. But when we write or speak or act without preplanning, what is it that actually happens? How does the mind form the process by which a matter comes to the fore? Or put another way, how do we prioritise? I am nervous of looking at this and committing pen to paper because my conscious mind holds no answer to the question at this moment. Of course, I could step in to exercise control at any time, to direct the process but I recognise that that would be pointless. The reason for doing this is to remove the control of my conscious mind. Even the reassurance of knowing I could intervene weakens the effect.

So I have to ask myself the most challenging of questions: why do we need to feel a sense of control?

Is this need universal? Do you feel it too? Why does 'not being in control' feel unsafe when, in reality, we have little or no control over anything that truly matters?

By now you may be thinking that this is nonsense – that it is obvious why we need to feel safe and therefore be in control. You may be ready to throw in the towel, dump this irritating little book onto the nearest bookshelf or rubbish pile and find something more useful to read, such as a workshop manual or tonight's TV listings. But now we are right back to that knotty problem of exactly how we form our preferences and priorities. How we decide what to draw towards us or push away from us. Because we draw towards us what is comfortable, familiar, engaging, we drive away what is threatening, boring, uncomfortable.

So here we are now, right at the centre of the conundrum. And the only question that remains is, will you, will I, choose to be in the moment, however pleasant or unpleasant, however comfortable or uncomfortable, however much ease or dis-ease it generates? For in the moment lies the gateway to consciousness itself.

May you hold the moment all through the day today– in the queue at the traffic lights when you're late for your appointment; when the computer is spinning little circles while it decides whether to follow your instructions or not; when your two-year-old is nagging for attention in the supermarket queue. Hold the moment, look at the emotions that arise, that drive your choices, and see what happens.

33 When Ink Turns To Blood

Back at the table after a few intensive days spent signing books for my lovely readers, I am confronted by the fact that I have omitted to place a black pen in my bag before setting out for the café.

Fortunately, the red pen I use for correcting my own work is here, so that's what I'm using to write today. It's different. It's a little harsher on the eye. It also carries connotations from the past.

Unnumbered armies of schoolteachers used the red pen to correct the submissions of hopeful or hopeless children. A well-placed, thoughtful red remark can elevate a young mind, gently steering it in the direction of growth. An angry, sarcastic comment in oversized letters can convey disdain, dismissal – an implied devaluation to the point of worthlessness. A red pen can express more incandescent rage than an angry face – if you know how to use it, that is; if you still occupy that space in which you feel the need to hurt other people, particularly those who are weaker than you.

It brings to mind the time at age ten when my parents arranged for me to receive private tuition in English and maths in the hope that it would increase my chances of being selected for grammar school.

On the first day of attendance at the enormous home belonging to the husband-and-wife tutor team, I knew I was in for trouble. The wife asked me if I had done fractions. I said yes but I made a mistake in giving that answer. She said fractions. I actually meant decimals. I didn't know the difference. *Try these,* she said, setting out a few fraction sums in my exercise book – 9/5 x 4//7, or some such. It might have been a Martian inscription for all I knew. I had never seen such things before. The tutor returned half an hour later to my untouched fractions. Her face reddened and contorted into an apoplectic rage. *You've not done this before have you?* She screamed. *Why did you lie to me, you stupid little boy?* Were those her actual words? Possibly not, but the emotion I feel as I write this in teacherly red ink is real to the point of being physically tangible. I fought back the tears until the end of the hour, then as soon as I got into my mother's little red Austin Mini I exploded into a wail of grief. I swore that I would never enter that house again. I swore that I didn't care which school I went to. I swore that nothing else mattered than to avoid a repetition of the abuse I had just suffered at the hands of a paid tutor.

Well, words were had. A promise of gentler treatment was extracted and I did return. Neither of them abused me again but, sadly, the warning had no impact whatsoever on the way they treated other children. I sat there one Saturday morning as a mild-mannered, compliant little girl handed in some work that was deemed marginally unsatisfactory. Bad! the bearded husband wrote on the work – fortunately in pencil. The little girl coloured up. Tears began to well up in her eyes. *Her father will have a fit,* commented the wife. *Really?* replied the husband in a jocular tone. *Then her mother can have a fit too.* He rubbed out 'Bad' and proceeded to fill a complete page of this defenceless little child's exercise book with a scrawled 'VERY BAD!!!' I remember particularly the three exclamation marks. The little girl's response was predictable. She exploded into loud, violent sobs, her body shaking, as geysers of grief rose up inside her. She wept and wept and would not stop. *That's enough!* said the wife in an authoritarian tone. But the little girl's weeping was uncontrollable and continued unabated.

The tutors looked at each other and then at the clock, as it approached the witching hour of midday, when the two hours of so-called tuition ended. *All right, all right,* said the husband in a somewhat gentler tone. *I didn't really mean it. Here, look. I'll rub it out.* The pencil marks were duly removed. *Here, have a sweet,* he said, as if an infusion of sugar could have the same impact on the little girl's heart as his eraser had had on the pencilled comments. But wounds inflicted on the psyche are never easily erased. Like pencil marks on paper, they leave lasting indentations that change the page forever.

I wonder, now, what happened when that child got into her mother or father's car. What grief was wept as she doubled over in the agony of failure and disappointment, abused by someone she might have expected to be able to trust? What discussion was held in her home as she unquestionably continued her inconsolable crying through that lunch hour? I'm guessing a decision was arrived at quite quickly that day, for I never saw her again, though I continued to attend for tuition in the home of those so-called teachers for several months after that.

I was going to go on from here to tell you about an abusive comment I was subjected to at the Dorset Show this weekend. But that will have to wait until another day. Right now, I'm too filled with compassion for that child from all those years ago to want to move on to a different subject. I don't know if she was accepted into grammar school or not. I don't know if she became a compulsive eater as I did, from the use of sugar to deaden her pain. But I am certain that she carried that grief in her heart for many years to come; that she was driven by an inner urge to please others, particularly authority figures and significant others. And I rather think she has spent too many of her years carrying a deep yet unconscious inconsolable grief.

We may not always know the reason for our behaviour. But we can be certain that without exception it invariably has a cause. Be careful today if you are tempted to take out your metaphorical red pen to correct or admonish another. It is a sword that you wield and it stabs so deep. When you withdraw it, you will find that the ink has turned to blood.

34 I'll Meet You In The Field

Some days it can be difficult to get here. I don't mean get to the café because I am writing at my desk this morning and I can write anywhere if I put my mind to it. And that's the key. I can do pretty much anything if I apply myself.

All the excuses I make; all the obstacles I put in my own way – the appointments in my diary, the household chores, the people around me, bless their dear hearts, the emails, notifications, special not-to-be-missed, one-day-only offers. All such things are vying for my attention and it is so, so easy for me to put them first. I can prioritise my day away until, finally, I collapse in a heap in front of some mindless Netflix offering that in all probability I will not remember tomorrow and certainly will be long gone from my memory by the end of the year. I can prioritise the writing of books and the signing of books and the selling of books and I can prioritise the organisation of the signing and selling of books.

For I am prone to prioritising what gives me enjoyable, reassuring feedback from what tells me I am doing something useful in the world or what brings me enjoyment. I can prioritise my life away with distraction, reach my final breath on my final day on the planet and look back and say, yep, I sold a lot of books. I watched a lot of TV. I can even look back and convince myself I did a certain amount of good, maybe even a lot of good.

Or, I can stop and take a deep breath. Then I can take another one. And if I permit myself, I can take a whole series of deep breaths, focusing on the moment, addressing my attention to the stillness that surrounds my breath, the stillness that is all about me when I clamour with thoughts of how many books I will sell, or what the outcome of the war in Sudan might be, or whether I should be acting any differently from what I am doing right now.

And all that time, the stillness is there, just being, as from it arises every thought that hovers for a moment before evaporating back into emptiness, every selfish or goodwill intention, every act aimed at reassuring myself of my value, every physical construct, every object made of atomic particles, every electron that spins around them, making up a physical universe that is dancing, waltzing its way about an infinite ballroom of emptiness that some call love.

And I can preoccupy myself with anything and everything that is not love, that is not emptiness, until I choose to stop and draw that breath and then another, until I decide to let it all go and let the emptiness that is love have me back.

In his poem A Great Wagon[9], the Sufi poet, Rumi, said, *Out beyond ideas of wrongdoing and rightdoing there is a field. I'll meet you there.* I don't think there is any grass in Rumi's field. And I know a little more now, about what he meant by meeting me there.

35 Beautiful

I took a new bar of soap from the bathroom cabinet this morning. On the box was written the statement 'Beauty Bar'. I smiled, wryly, as I withdrew the soap from the box. The words suggest the link the manufacturer wants me to make between their product and some nefarious concept of beauty that the user might hope to attain by washing with it.

We could devote a great deal of time, should we be so inclined, to the matter of the continual assaults that the advertising industry makes on our thinking, seeking to make this or that product desirable, seeking to convince us that what is offered will help us to become more like what we want to be – or perhaps to delay the time when we cease to be what we already like being. But I am more interested in this moment in what it is that we perceive to be beautiful. A sunset, maybe? A forest panorama in autumn colour? A human body of a particular age, sex, or shape? Much philosophical debate has been expended on the question of whether beauty is objective or subjective. But at the heart of the matter lies the question of what it is that moves us towards something we considered desirable, what captivates the senses when we first perceive it.

I stop writing at this point (which I'm not supposed to do until I finish), lost for something to say. The words do not flow easily; perhaps because I have focused my mind on a philosophical issue rather than letting go. That's a profound lesson in itself and one that I will not deprive you of by destroying this piece before it reaches the printed page. It reminds me that I am not here to impress you with how clever a writer I am, or how spiritually advanced I am. I do this for one reason only: to illuminate spiritual journeys, both yours and mine. And sometimes on that journey we take a wrong turn that leads to a dead end, or worse. Then there is nothing for it but to back up to the crossroads and take another path.

This morning on the news there was a report on the 15,000 amputees that have reached Ukrainian hospitals in the last six months, having lost limbs and more due to the war. The article focused on a young man, in his twenties, I estimated, who had lost most of both arms and been blinded in both eyes, his face horribly scarred. Many seeing that, me included, would have concluded it was something of a blessing that he will never be able to see his own face again. Until, that was, the camera turned to his pretty young wife sat close by him, body pressed against body, hands held tight, looking into that disfigured face, declaring that she loved him even more now, for his determination, for his indomitable spirit. The article finished with his statement that his greatest sadness was not his personal loss but his inability to finish the job that he had started for his country.

That young woman saw beauty in her husband's disfigured face every time she looked at him. No doubt there will be traumas ahead for them as first he regains movement, voice, strength, and then as he passes such other milestones as he proves capable of. Then there will be the emotional elements, perhaps including PTSD, as they both come to terms with loss, as they determine where their lives will lead, where they will lead their lives.

I don't think that young woman will be much concerned with beauty bars for a while now. I don't think she will be too bothered which soap offers her more chance of achieving an oversold, superficial concept of loveliness.

In Ode on a Grecian Urn[10], John Keats declares

Beauty is truth, truth beauty - that is all
Ye know on earth and all ye need to know.

I'll try to remember that as I go about my day, seeking

to strip away the layers of superficiality from my perception and behaviour; not criticising or chastising myself for my failures, my inclination to be too easily deceived by what I am told. But simply panning for gold as it sparkles through the silt, when my eyes are open enough to see it. Nor will I be changing my preferred brand of soap any time soon. It is no bar to my being beautiful.

36 Muscle Man

I pulled a muscle yesterday when unloading a delivery of boxes of books onto the shelves in my garage. I picked up a box less carefully that I might have done. It toppled out of my hands, onto the pallet and from there onto the floor. As it fell I made a grab for it, overreaching myself and twisting a muscle in my lower back. The delivery driver who was helping me jumped out of the way as the box tumbled to the floor, then calmly picked it up and handed it back to me with a smile. Though I did not ask, it would not surprise me to learn that he was a practitioner of meditation. I apologised, a little embarrassed, and carried on loading the boxes onto the shelves, rather more carefully than I had done previously.

After the driver left, I looked at all the filled shelves with satisfaction. There is something about seeing the regularity of all the boxes lined up tidily that I find appealing. Beauty, as the phrase has it, is in the eye of the beholder. I enjoyed the moment to the extent that I was later tempted to go back and look at the boxes again. But the moment of unloading, that I did not enjoy so much.

I had planned the delivery carefully, arranging for a text to be sent to me in advance, so that I could look out for the lorry at the right time, since I often miss the doorbell. I had moved my car well out of the way so as to avoid any mishaps as the driver pulled the pallet truck up the drive. I had cleared the garage of anything that might impede or endanger the passage of the truck into an easy unloading position. But when the moment of unloading arrived, I wanted to get it over and done with as soon as possible, so I worked too quickly.

The boxes were not too heavy. I have long since received training in moving and handling technique, so I knew how to do the job safely. But I did not want to do it. The work was effort I did not want to expend. I anticipated that the moment after completion would be more enjoyable than the moment of the work itself. So I shifted my attention away from the moment of work and onto my representation of the future, more enjoyable, moment. But that future moment was not real. The only reality at the moment of unloading was the unloading itself. My attachment to desire took me out of that moment and into my fantasy of the future. My lack of attention to the moment resulted in an accident, albeit a minor one.

All of that, of course, happened in an instant without conscious thought. But the learning for me here lies in accepting all moments as they are, not trying to make them into something I would prefer them to be. Appropriate concentration would have avoided a harmful consequence – one I am living with now as I write this, since I have spent the last 24 hours with backache. That will pass, as do all moments. I accept it as it is. Instead of trying to avoid the pain, I look into the pain. I locate it in my body. I consider clearly and closely the nature of it. I examine what I mean by pain, why I find the sensation of it unpleasant. I consider all those thoughts and emotions that I usually use to surround and insulate myself from pain or unpleasantness: the self-criticism and judgement for my thoughtlessness, the regret that I was not more careful, the hope that the pain will pass quickly. All of it amounts to representation of the past or future, or an alternative but fictitious present that I think I would find more palatable. Then I return to the present, accept the moment and thank it for the learning it brings. And I remind myself that there is no suffering in the pain itself.

'There is the cause of suffering,' says the second of the Buddha's Four Noble Truths, 'which is the attachment to desire.' I allow myself to meditate on this, one of the most radical statements on suffering ever made. Is it literally true? I am not certain in this moment of pain. But what I do know is that I suffer less when I release my attachment to desire.

May you be happy. May you and all beings, me included, be free from suffering.

37 Change Is A-Foot

I first came to New Milton in 1996 and have had connections with the town on and off ever since. A lot has changed on the High Street in that time – supermarkets have been rebranded, pubs have disappeared with a decline in social drinking. One in particular, The Trout, was demolished to make way for the new health centre. The second-hand furniture traders have given way to the chain-franchised Costa café where I am writing today. But crossing the railway bridge as I walked into town this morning gave me a glimpse further back into the past.

A pine furniture retailer has given up in the face of Internet competition. Its trading unit, immediately opposite the station, has been boarded up, presumably to prevent vandalism, while plans for its future are advanced. In the process, the Perspex name board above the shop has been removed to reveal a much older, painted name above the unit – that of Cecil G Foot. Peeling painted letters on a discoloured tan background give a clue to the vintage of the sign, which I guessed to be about 100 years old.

Intrigued, I researched Mr Foot online and was quickly rewarded with several historical articles detailing both who he was and the history of the large retail unit concerned. Cecil Foot was an estate agent and auctioneer who took possession of the shop in 1928. But he was also well-known for refusing to take up arms to kill in the First World War. However, no white feathers for cowardice came Cecil's way, for he was awarded a medal for valour in his role as a stretcher-bearer.

So, Mr Foot saved lives, he survived his war service, he traded, he lived, and he died. And though his legacy was recorded in the local history books it has taken almost 100 years for his name to reappear once more on the hoarding above his shop. Mr Foot has, as it were, risen from the grave to re imprint his name on the psyche of the town.

Shops come and go. Generations pass. Change is ubiquitous, happening all around us so continuously that from moment to moment we barely notice. And the same level of change that is taking place all around us is also taking place within us. 90% of all cells in our body are replaced each year. Even the least frequently renewed are replaced within 15 years.

I am, quite literally, not the same person I was last year. I retain a sense of continuity by way of memory of past events, accurate or otherwise – energy patterns lodged in my brain that convinced me that, though Michael might have a few more grey hairs or a few more aches and pains than he did five years ago, he is essentially the same person. For the most part, we quite simply cannot cope without the sense of identity, of ego that memory gives us. For if I am not *Michael, son of Leonard, 68 years of age, with all his personal history, his education, qualifications, profession, children, grandchildren and life events*, then exactly who am I?

Most of us cannot deal with the uneasiness brought by awareness that we might not be who we think we are. Most simply choose to ignore the glaringly obvious facts of universal inconsistency until they stand in front of us, shake us by the shoulders and spit in our eye. Instead it's *Yes, well I do change, of course, but I am obviously the same person I was 20, 30, 40 years ago. I still like reading, travelling, stimulating conversation and good movies. All that means, surely, that I am me.*

We ignore it until we can't. Until a plan-disrupting life event – a birth, a death, an illness, confronts us with the reality that life not only begins and ends but is beginning and ending every moment of our conscious awareness. And then, if we are willing to listen, we realise that our identities are as leaves on an enduring oak. They are brought into being as the tree exudes its life into us in spring. They brighten and thrive in the summer warmth and light and wane as the tree draws back its energy in autumn. They shrivel and fall to feed the Earth when the illusion of our independent identity is drawn back into the tree. We continue being what we always were – the energy of the tree, not the flimsy form of leaf or ego that contains it.

Cecil had his day. Traces of his energy lingered silently behind a plastic name board that hung above his shop for 80 years more. And with the passing of that identity, the echo of his voice is still there for those that have ears to hear. It speaks of the illusion of permanence and the inevitability of transience. Thank you, Cecil. Because you are still speaking, I will spend my time more beneficially today.

38 It's Not My Fault

I have removed my cochlear hearing device to be able to write without distraction this morning. There are not many advantages to being deaf and in particular to being a cochlear implant wearer but one that can be useful is the ability to eliminate noise distraction instantly. As soon as I remove the device from the side of my head, I become even more aware how noisy the environment is around me– how loudly people speak to one another in order to overcome the impact of the hubbub created by their own raised voices.

And herein lies an interesting lesson: that which we do individually for innocent enough reasons, when aggregated to the collective level, can have an unintended and disproportionate impact. One person tearing a wrapper off a sandwich looks around and sees no bin, so drops the waste on the ground. It might be irritating to watch, but as an individual act it has little impact. But if ten thousand do the same thing in Wembley Stadium it takes an army of litter pickers and a convoy of refuse trucks to carry away the discarded waste after a game. And if ten million do it across the country or a billion do it across the world, it fills landfill sites, clogs the waterways, destroys the environment and kills species.

When I was a child, I was taught to put my litter in the bin or take it home with me. Now, if I visit the local recreation ground on a Sunday morning after a sunny Saturday afternoon, the skate park is covered with discarded drink containers and food wrappers, not to mention the occasional bent bike wheel or broken skateboard. I look up at the observation cameras that stare down from the top of 10-metre poles, wondering who in the control room observes the action and chooses to do nothing about it.

Along comes the street cleaner with brush and shovel and in an hour the park is back to its pristine state. It is his job to clear up the mess and my job to pay his wages through my council tax. But it is seemingly no one's job to prevent it happening in the first place – not the teenager dropping the litter (and yes, I know older people sometimes do the same thing), not the parents who failed to teach their child social responsibility, not the police who have more important tasks overwhelming them.

At the collective level, we commonly fail to take

responsibility for the perpetration of acts, preferring to accept the consequences of acts. We see the same principle in retail, where only relatively recently has attention begun to be paid to the recycling of packaging. And even now, as I unpack my shopping at home, it is instantly noticeable how little of the packaging can actually be placed in the recycling bin.

The same principle also applies to unhealthy lifestyles. As a society we have failed to control the unending rollout of fast-food outlets, until every High Street is garishly dominated by burger joints, pizza houses, fried chicken retailers and vendors of high calorie drinks. Almost all of us have failed to see the expansion of our collective waistline, preferring to worship at the deceptively named shrine of consumer choice (for which, regrettably you can often substitute produce manipulation).

All of us, that is, except for the medical fraternity, whose job it is mop up the consequences of those so-called choices – in particular, the obesity epidemic that threatens to devastate our already overwhelmed public health service. And still we insist on our right to make unwise choices, to act with impunity, to ignore the collective consequences of our planet-wide enslavement to the claims of addictions that are rarely named as such which suit the preferences of the manufacturers of addictive food and non-food products.

What will it take to bring change? In the next ten

or twenty years the chorus of demand for solutions will rise to a deafening crescendo. Save us from our fat. Save us from our clogged lungs, our clogged arteries, our clogged waterways. It's not my fault I have become like this. It's someone else's fault, and anyway, it's my right to live as I choose. It's your obligation to set me free of the consequences of my choices. And if you don't agree, come the election some other politician will agree – or at least will purport to agree and promise a solution, until the next crisis of the immediate has driven the worry from our collective mind.

Save us from ourselves and the consequences of our actions but on no account tell us we are responsible. And never, never tell us that we need to change our behaviour. Don't remind us not to drop litter. Don't confront us with what vaping is doing to our lungs. Don't keep telling us what excess calories are doing to our hearts and other organs. Because that's just uncomfortable noise and all we have to do when we are distracted by it is to take off our collective hearing device and luxuriate in the joy of self-delusional silence.

39 No Place Like Home

I'm on the train to London this morning so please excuse me if my handwriting is difficult to read (!). I'm familiar with this trip, taking it frequently to meet friends and family. But I don't take it nearly as often as I did in my 20s, when, for two separate periods of around nine months each, I was a daily commuter.

I would walk to the station for the 7:43 (or whatever), stand on a densely packed platform and then be carried forward with the human tide surging onto the train. I lived in the North London suburbs on both occasions, so the train coming from Luton, or Welwyn, or wherever, was always relatively full before it arrived at my stop. There was rarely a chance to sit for the forty-minute journey. Sometimes a train would be cancelled, in which case twice as many people would try to cram onto the next one. Tinned sardines had more breathing space than we

144

commuters did. We were pressed together into unwanted intimacy without regard for age or sex. We tolerated it only because there was no alternative and only because it was for a relatively short, predictable time.

But even at such a time, when our environment was well beyond our control, we managed it, as humans are prone to doing. Though we had no control over posture or position, proximity or preference, we always had eye control. Many closed their eyes; most averted them. The few that chose to do otherwise commonly were either travelling with companions they knew well, or in a very few cases, seemed to derive a sense of power from causing discomfort by looking directly into the eyes of others.

Anonymity is relatively easy to maintain when we refrain from eye contact. Walk down the street in any sizeable town and only rarely will someone coming the other way connect with you eye-to-eye. The more densely we live together, the less we want to acknowledge one another. We cede our sense of individuality in an overcrowded commuter train or a busy street, arriving with relief at the office to occupy a familiar desk, or at least one that we personify temporarily, with family photos, a personal computer, a lucky charm. The space becomes our own, an extension of ourselves in the same way as a home, or a car can do. In our personalised space we revert to an individuality that is difficult to maintain in places where we feel no sense of ownership or power.

Does a generation forced into renting a home instead of owning it feel a diminished sense of identity? Do displaced persons lose their sense of self-worth for lack of a place to call home? Do warring nations sacrifice life and limb in the pursuit of space that calls something indefinable out from the heart of them?

We identify with place. Our selfhood is intimately associated with our space of origin. Threaten that space, threaten to take it away from us and we become aggressive or fearful. We grow to love the land not because it is intrinsically beautiful but because we project our identity onto it.

For almost thirty years now, I have lived in and around The New Forest. I have loved the land and it has loved me. Yet in the last year or so, a sense of detachment has been growing within me. I still find joy in the Forest. I still derive learning beyond measure from this, my greatest teacher in this lifetime. But as I have learned to recognise that I am not my body and my mind but something that encompasses both, I feel a lesser need to attach to the space I occupy. There are not too many more years left to pass before I will relinquish land and mind and body. Great joy will transition with me for the privilege of having occupied all of these. But none of them have been home.

40 Go Wrestle

What do you fear most? I stared at the question on my screen. There was no one here asking it in person so no one to impress with a clever answer. This was an opportunity with no impurity – nothing to distract me from honesty, nothing to prevent me from seeing my own truth. I sat, looking at that question for several minutes, searching through my undisclosed fears – all those nightmare possibilities I will not discuss with anyone, for fear that they would think less of me.

Was that it? I wondered. Was my greatest fear that I would lose status, lose face, as a result of honest disclosure? I thought not. In this world, in this time, there are and always will be people who think highly of you and others who are dismissive of your worth – commonly because of what they feel about themselves, their own issues that they are here to deal with in this particular lifetime. And those high and low opinions, they will rise and fall like the passing of the seasons. *Treat those two impostors just the same,* wrote Rudyard Kipling of triumph and disaster in the poem 'If[11].' For opinion is empty, illusionary – here for a moment then gone with the generation. There are deeper concerns to fear.

I delved deeper inside myself in search of an answer to that most searching of questions. I wanted to get up and walk away from the screen. No one would know if I decided to avoid the issue – if I stuffed it back down into my psyche and pretended I had never seen it. Heck, I could probably even convince myself that I had not seen it or could not think of an answer – at least for long enough to forget while some other preoccupation rose up to distract me. But if I failed to answer it now, it would always be there, sitting like a monk in the lotus position, assuming nothing, waiting until I decided to return to it.

If not this question, then which other is more important? If the time to address it is not now, then when? I did not get up. I sat, staring at the screen, wondering what the answer might be. A vicious dog cornering me? A random madman with a knife bursting into the room where I sat? Staring down the barrel of a terrorist's gun? I do not know how I would react to any of these were they to happen. I am not easy with the possibility that I might well not conduct myself with honour when confronted with something life-threatening. But I do not know and will not know until such a moment occurs, if it ever does.

So I sat on, finally facing the question I did not want to face, finally taking that question in an arm lock and wrestling with it, finally stepping past my fear of the answer in my determination to know what that answer was.

Tell me your name, I might have cried, as did the biblical Jacob, when he wrestled with that unknown man through the night. On they fought, grappling with each other until the sun began to rise over the horizon. Sweat drenched and ragged, battled to the dirt in the weariness of it, the unnamed man touched Jacob in the hollow of his thigh, such that for the rest of his years he limped, always reminded of his greatest battle. Every external conflict he ever faced during his long life after that was as nothing, a mere distraction from the great business of discovering and naming the man. Finally, when they were done, just as the sun's rays licked at their feet, the assailant left him, and Jacob knew he had wrestled with God.

And me? Oh yes I got my answer, sitting in front of the screen. I even typed it, watching the letters form a single word that I looked at long and deep, touched in the hollow of my own thigh by the awareness that I had gained. And no, I will not be sharing the answer with you today. I have a much more important question to leave you with instead:

What is it that you fear most?

Go wrestle.

41 Illusion

What happens when we change locations?

We have changed the venue for Writing Practice today from our usual Costa café in New Milton to the Boston Tea Party in Ringwood. All around me in the café full English breakfasts rub shoulders with sweet corn hash and smashed avocado on sourdough toast. In front of me on the slatted wooden table, tin cans hold cutlery and napkins. Now that we have finished eating, to my side stands the detritus of two much enjoyed breakfasts (only the one was mine, you understand), the remains of a steaming mug of coffee and an empty pot of Oolong Tea. Breakfast is over. Now we write.

As I settle, letting the environment seep into me, I realise that yes, there is a different atmosphere here, even in the silence, with my hearing processor removed. Mind you, it's not the silence that is different – that is

150

universal. When you meditate and allow yourself to find that silence, the first thing you notice is simply that it is there. For silence is not simply the absence of sound. It is a state in its own right. It has not just started because you have stopped prioritising the noise and are focusing on the moment. It was there before you started contemplating it. It has always been there. It will always be there.

This silence is the steady, unheard heartbeat of the universe that you are tuning into, the foundation that underpins all that you see, or hear, or feel in the world of apparent material substance. And if you go on maintaining your awareness and focus, you gradually become aware that the silence is everything. 'Emptiness' as Zen practitioners sometimes term it, is the flipside of substance. The table I am writing on is solid, substantial. It holds up the blue, ring-bound notebook in which I am writing. It holds the coffee mug by my left hand. Yet contemplate it long enough, stay in the moment long enough, and you realise something astonishing: that the table is illusory, the ring binder is emptiness, the pen is nothing. They are here and not here at the same time. They and the words that I form all spring out of the silence, communicate their meaning, then fade away again into the emptiness. Go on contemplating it and you realise that the emptiness is you; that you are the emptiness.

Am I here? Assuredly – as certainly as you are there. But allow your awareness to stay in the moment long enough and you are awakened to the reality that we are not who we think we are. The mind that conjures our identities itself springs from the emptiness and returns to it. Moment by moment, reality is being formed.

Is this confusing? Most of us find it so when we first encounter it. Perhaps confusion, uncertainty, and the openness of Beginner's Mind that are characterised by them are the best place to come from. Releasing our hold on knowledge, we move towards understanding; we begin to learn to abandon the fiction of that hold we thought we had on the universe, and see ourselves for the reality of what we are.

42 When Expectations Differ

I own a rental flat in a block. Yesterday, the person that manages the block announced that there was water penetrating three floors down from my flat, coming from an unknown source. Could everyone please be there tomorrow said the email (i.e. today), to let the plumber in to check where the leak is coming from. I had no other commitments for today so I emailed back 'Sure. What time?' and then heard nothing more. This morning at about 10:30 am I received another email: 'He'll be there any time between 10.00 am and 12.00 noon.' My instant response was irritation. 'If he thinks I'm waiting around for two hours for someone to arrive at their leisure, he can forget it!' I thought. I was really put out at the presumptuousness of it. Why was the manager's time and/or the plumber's time more important than my time? Particularly when I'm only told the possible time range for the visit half an hour into the period concerned?

Then I stopped, let the irritation dissipate and allowed myself to settle. From a more centred state I gave the matter clearer thought. I cannot change the manager's presumptuousness. I cannot change the plumber's schedule. I cannot change the fact that it is now, at the time of writing, an hour into his two-hour window. In fact, I cannot actually be there at all. The source of the leak will be found or will not be found. Given that my flat is one of 24 in the block, the chances are that I am not going to be needed anyway. The chances are that several other owners or tenants will also not be able to attend. The problem will either get solved or the visit will be rescheduled.

I cannot change any of that. But what I can change is my own reaction – my sense of entitlement, that I am due more courtesy than I am being given; my sense of diminution and my irritation are being treated as unimportant in my own estimation. And when all is said and done, the only person that really affects is me. In a very real and practical sense, I am creating my own suffering by attaching to the desire to be treated in a particular way. I am hurting myself by protecting my ego.

The only way I can make myself suffer less and make the world a little better, is by letting go of my beliefs about what I am entitled to. And that is a pretty good conclusion to have arrived at and a pretty good place to stop writing today.

May all beings be happy. Including thoughtless managers and over-busy plumbers. May they be happy. And me, of course. 'All beings' includes me. May I be happy too.

43 Wounded Surgeons

The phrase, 'A Nice Little Book of Poems' was mentioned to me literally as I picked up my pen to write this morning. My partner – the poet Jacqueline Haskell – had her first poetry collection, *Stroking Cerberus*[12], published by Myriad Editions just as we headed into lockdown in 2020. Myriad, as is normal for a traditional publisher, allocated a budget to marketing and duly publicised the book in the lead up to the launch, which was held in Waterstones, Brighton. Many congratulatory comments came Jacqui's way from other published and aspiring poets. The poetry community is not large and many know one another. But someone in that community came back with a comment to the effect that it was good to see her nice little book of poems published.

If ever there was a comment intended to patronise, to deflate and diminish, this was it. It carried a sense of malicious superiority that I remember from school by unsupportive teachers slapping down enthusiastic pupils. Then again in my early career, where seniors deprecated the efforts of juniors. All through my life I have seen it and so, probably, have you. Hierarchical structures where power is asserted by people in actual or self-perceived positions of authority, who feel the need to belittle others in order to make themselves feel superior. Where it comes from we can only speculate – perhaps a child who has been crushed by significant others goes on to reassert their own sense of self-worth by crushing someone weaker or smaller in their turn. Perhaps we all undertake both roles at different times in our lives – the crushed and the crusher – in an endless cycle of destructiveness that ensures the psychological scarring of each new generation, carrying the sins of the fathers onto the children until the third and fourth generation.

Until, that is, we see it and make the active decision to break the cycle. Until we choose to build up someone we perceive to be weaker, rather than break them down. Until we choose to encourage rather than discourage. Until we choose to heal rather than hurt, to bind up the wounds of the broken to permit that healing, rather than grinding dirt into their open sores.

We need to understand that we must do this before our own wounds are fully healed. We have to make that decision to reach out in kindness to someone in need at precisely the moment when we could do with encouragement ourselves. But you know what? When you do, you discover that your act of loving-kindness becomes a salve to heal your own wounds. In binding the broken you are healing yourself.

May today be a healing day. May I be a wounded physician who heals himself through acts of kindness towards those around me that really need it – and that of course is everyone.

And that nice little book of poems, *Stroking Cerberus*? Jacqueline Haskell read from it in front of hundreds who attended the launch that night. There was standing room only and they stood all the way up the stairs to the second floor. Afterwards, the till rang out for hours to the sound of purchases made by a queue of buyers that stretched out beyond my line of sight.

Not bad for a nice little book of poems.

44 A Thinning Of The Veil

In Café Zero, the cobwebs are hanging thick on the front of the counter. I am tempted to tell the baristas to have a word with the cleaner – but it would only be in jest. I am back in Glastonbury at Samhain – Halloween, if you're not a pagan. The date marks the beginning of the Celtic New Year. At this time, the veil between the living and the dead is said to be especially thin, facilitating the entry of spirits into this tangible world – if you're a Wiccan or a pagan, that is, or if you have a propensity to connect to this unseen world anyway.

I too am a seer of 'ghosts' and of the unseen world, even though I am not a pagan and do not see spirits. But I connect to what is unseen whenever I allow myself to look past the superficial presentation of the visible world – the buildings and the bodies, the haunted egos grasping at wispy ghosts of satisfaction, past the stress and suffering

159

caused by attachment to desire and the preferring of the self. And when I do, I awaken first to my own awareness and then to the silence, the spirit, or God, if you will, to that which lies below the superficiality that we so easily prioritise. When I do so, when I really let go, I am reminded of how little it all matters – the ambition, the ownership, the craving for status and recognition that drove my motives and actions for so long. Now that I acknowledge silence, I am also blessed with the learning that sufficient is always enough and that very little is often sufficient.

I do not mean this in a callous, patronising way, you understand, not in self-satisfaction. For the more I occupy this space of awareness, the more conscious I become of need and suffering around me – the psychological suffering by those who prioritise ego, certainly, but also the very real physical suffering of the many, many people who go without and suffer physically daily. That bag lady who was the first person I noticed on walking into town this morning; the people in this morning's newscast from Israel and Gaza, aching with the pain of fear and destruction and loss on both sides of the border; the overwhelming number that launch flimsy dinghies from the coast of North Africa, sold a fictitious dream of safety and gold-paved streets in a Europe whose ability to absorb them has all but collapsed, and which is now, increasingly, looking for a means of turning them away.

I cannot meditate alone in my room and then emerge

into a world of such overwhelming need without reaching out to that suffering. I cannot tell a bag lady with an empty belly to detach from her desire. I cannot tell a fleeing Eritrean man to meditate in order to release himself from his suffering. I cannot tell a hungry young farmer in Borneo to stop working for the palm oil company because he is damaging the planet. I cannot do any of this without taking action, without gifting my energy, be it financially or by way of my time, or my voice, or any other method available to me.

The deeper I go, the thinner the veil becomes. And the veil I am talking about is not between the physical world and the spirit world. It is the one between you and me, him and me, her and me, them and me. If my awareness of our oneness, of our non-duality means anything, it has to mean that I reach out in an embrace of giving, as I let the energy and resources flow to where they are needed, to where the suffering is greatest.

This is Wicca. This is paganism. This is Buddhism. This is Islam. This is Christianity. This is humanism. The veil is so thin between them all. On this Samhain I redouble my dedication to reach across it.

45 Standing In The Road

Three days ago, on the 5th of November, the United Kingdom celebrated Guy Fawkes' Night. The rear of my house faces towards a school just across the copse and the meadow from us. We can usually rely on a colourful display, however I might feel about the trauma it carries for animal life, both domestic and wild. The school had scheduled its display for the 4th of November, being a Saturday. I was driving home from an event that evening, so I did not actually get to see any coloured lights in the sky.

But what I did pass as I neared home, were hordes of people heading away from the school after the event. Most were careful to steer clear of the traffic, but once I turned off the main road by the side of the lake, that care seemed to have fizzled out along with the fireworks. Groups of people were making their way up the pavement, spilling onto the road, oblivious to the potential consequences, presuming, if they thought about it at all, that the road would be as safe as the pavement. Further along, a group was standing in the road chatting, seemingly put out that a driver actually wanted to pass. I slowed to the proverbial snail's pace and passed within centimetres of people's arms and legs. Still they continue chatting and laughing, still they spilled out onto the road, eschewing the safety of the pavement, perceiving no risk.

Enjoying ourselves relaxes us. Relaxing can insulate us from any sense of potential danger, without, of course, insulating us from danger itself. Sometimes there is every reason to think we are safe. Regrettably, sometimes not.

During Ramadan 2011, tourists – mostly British – were lying on Sousse Beach in Tunisia sipping cocktails and soaking up the sun, dipping themselves in the sea when they became too hot. There was no reason to think of danger. This was a safe beach in a safe country, well away from the world's trouble spots. Until, that was, an Islamic State terrorist carried onto that beach a rifle concealed under a parasol. He emptied his magazine into the terrified tourists, killing 39 and maiming a further 36.

On 7th October 2023, a music festival took place in the Negev desert in Israel, some 5 km from the border with Gaza. Shall we go or shan't we? mused the festivalgoers. Some, no doubt, leaned to caution and deemed the location too much of a risk. Some took the view that all had been quiet for a long time in Gaza. *Hamas busies itself with the task of governing,* some thought. Others gave the matter no thought. And anyway the world-renowned Israeli Defence Force would protect them. There would be no trouble at the festival. All would be well. And it was, until masked Hamas terrorists or freedom fighters (depending on which side of the divide you place yourself) burst from concealed tunnels and flew in on radar-evading hang gliders to unleash indiscriminate and deliberate slaughter on anyone they encountered, regardless of age, sex, nationality, or religion. In that instant all Israel awoke to the fact that what was presumed to be safe was far from the safe. One thousand four hundred were butchered that day. The Israelis later showed a video of the results to carefully selected and pre-warned journalists. So barbaric were the scenes it depicted, that many in attendance said they etched everlasting memories on their minds.

The Israeli response, when it came, seemed only a little less indiscriminate. Nowhere near enough time was permitted to evacuate a population numbered in millions before an unremitting hurricane of bombs and rockets fell from the sky, obliterating buildings, cars, roads, and humans of all ages, both sexes and several nationalities, together with some terrorists who were the declared targets.

In one of several similar stories, this morning's BBC News carried an item focusing on the story of a surgeon in Gaza, interrupted during surgery to be told that his children, his mother and others dear to him, had been killed in an overnight rocket strike. I understand why he took a risk himself, but why did he not evacuate his family? Presumably because he considered the risk of doing so to be greater than the risk of leaving them where they were.

'We have no other means of drawing the plight of our people to the world's attention than to hit Israel hard,' declared Hamas, with many silently believing that all Jews are vermin. 'We have no means of destroying the terrorists than to bomb, though there will be many civilians killed in the process,' declare the Israelis, with many silently believing that as a pseudo-nation the Palestinians had it coming, that the civilian Palestinian casualties were less important than the Israelis dead, maimed and kidnapped, who were caught up in the original atrocity.

After the war is over, declared Lt Col Blitch of the Israeli army, *there will still be Jews; there will still be Palestinians. We have to find a way of living with each other.*

As you wonder why it is that such a way could not have been found before the slaughter of the innocents, pray to your God that it will indeed be found and found quickly. For they are still standing in the road.

46 My New Shoes

I buy new shoes because my old ones are wearing out. There comes a point when, however comfortable the old pair, I acknowledge that they are approaching the end of their useful life. If I try to wear them for too long they will deteriorate rapidly, go into holes, start letting the water in on a wet day.

I head to the shoe shop, usually with little idea of what I am looking for beyond the fact that I want them to be comfortable, a good fit for me. I try on several pairs. Each feels strange to my habituated feet, which persistently ask to be returned to the shoes that are familiar. They want what they know, these feet of mine. They would wear the same shoes forever if they could.

But I know their comfort will not last as the old pair approach the end of their life. So, of all the pairs offered to me, I choose the one that feels the most right – the one that my intuition tells me will hold me best through my next steps. These new shoes have far to take me. I don't want to have to replace them again soon, if possible.

I make my choice and ask the shop assistant to put them into a bag. With some relief, I put my old, comfortable pair back on my feet. My feet are grateful. They did not enjoy the experience of newness and gravitate back to the familiar. But they know that change must come. They are reconciled to there being a last day that they will spend in those old shoes. Not yet, though. I am not asking them to relinquish their comfort with the old pair too suddenly. I will give them time to acclimatise to what is new, for I am considerate of my feet. I am grateful for their lifelong service. They have carried me far and we have yet some distance to travel together.

Back at home, the day comes to wear the new shoes for the first time. I step into them carefully, easing them on gently for they too must become used to what is at first unfamiliar. Shoes need as much time to adjust to feet as feet need to adjust to shoes. Then off we go. By the end of the day I will be grateful to remove them. What is new is hard work. Adjustment does not come easily. If the new shoes are particularly difficult to adjust to, I may even return to the old pair periodically, for short periods, as I ease my feet congruently into what is new. But I always know when the transition is complete. The moment always comes when that which was alien feels familiar, when my new shoes are as much a part of my journey as the old ones ever were.

And should I have cause to retain the old ones for occasional use in gardening or decorating, they will be the ones that feel unfamiliar. Why did I ever linger so long in these old shoes? I will ask myself. They are no longer a part of my journey. They hold memories of who I was when I wore them, for sure. But they are not for now. Not for this moment. Not for the future moments to come. My feet and I have moved on. Eventually, when they have no more relevance, I will drop them into the recycling bin. I will relinquish them respectfully, for they are a part of my past, a part of my journey that was. And in time they will return to the Earth from which they came. Though we remain grateful, my feet and I will not mourn them. We have new shoes. We have moved on.

47 Setting Off Alarms

Other than clothing, I wear nothing on my body beyond a red emergency wristband. In the event of my having an accident and being unable to speak, it shows that I am fitted with a cochlear implant, which would make it dangerous for me to be given an MRI scan.

When I pass through an airport security scanner, the metal part of the implant inside my head sometimes sets off the machine. So I am taken aside to receive a closer scan with a handheld device. Sometimes when that happens, I wonder what I must look like to the multitude of people passing through security and collecting their belongings on the conveyor. I imagine folk guessing at whether I am a drug smuggler or a terrorist. I have no aspirations to become either and have no guilty conscience. But nevertheless, I am always glad when I am released, and the security staff turn their attention elsewhere.

What must that job be like, I wonder? The need to remain constantly alert, to face daily the possibility that someone in the line might be trying to smuggle a weapon or a bomb onto an aircraft. The tension of the role must sometimes be overwhelming. And you can add to that any personal burdens the officer might be carrying that I will never know about. Then, inevitably, along comes the traveller who is themselves stressed: the nervous flyer fearing a crash, the disappointed would-be mother who has lost yet another embryonic child, the jilted lover, angry at the world. All are carrying their own personal trauma, managing it more or less well, depending on their capacity and the level of stress involved. It is not surprising that periodically someone lets out an angry response when they are already close to their limit and the apparent insensitivity of the security officer becomes one straw too many for their burdened back. How well it gets dealt with depends on the level of training the officer has received, the experience they have and the kind of stress they themselves have experienced that day.

We do our best to manage our conduct when our stress levels are low but when that tide rises too high it can wash over our flood barriers and result in conduct we later regret. That is not confined to airport security, of course. It can happen any day, anywhere, to us or to anyone else. We judge what we see in the moment, oblivious to the personal history that results in regrettable conduct. Each of us brings to every encounters our day's experience and our lifetime's experience. If I encounter you while I am in an unresourceful state today, distracted by what has been or what might yet be, I will have no way of knowing what sadness or disappointment, what hope and fears, you may be carrying. I hope I will be fully present when we meet. I hope I will make space for the whole person that is you. I hope I shall be what you need me to be. Today, I do not suppose I shall be setting off any security scanners. Nevertheless, I shall endeavour to be kind and understanding if you set off the alarm bells in me.

Go safely.

48 There's Nothing I Can Do

This last weekend I spent three days working flat out, signing books for my lovely readers in Salisbury. Given that we are in the final run-up to Christmas it's to be expected and I would not have it otherwise. One of the features of this particular event that intrigued me was the unusual level of interest in my ecological travelogue, *One Journey*. The book explores a variety of planetary concerns based on my first hand evidence, from deforestation in the Amazon Basin to Third World growth in Asia, particularly the Philippines.

Since it appeared in 2018, *One Journey* has been a relatively slow seller compared to some of my other books. But this year the book has been flying off the table. I am left to wonder as to what extent global fires and floods are increasing our awareness of what is happening to the planet on which we live.

Some of my more thoughtful readers will linger a long time and discuss the books with me at length before making their choice. One of the hundreds of people I spoke to on Sunday was a lady in late middle age who was especially interested in the ecological content of *One Journey*. This lovely lady did indeed buy a copy of the book but as she handed over of her payment there was a look of anguish on her face. *I wish I could do more, but I feel so helpless,* she said. And I have to say that sometimes I share her feeling of helplessness, so overwhelming is the task before us. I think we all do.

We appear now to have arrived at the position where it is impossible to think in terms of reducing global temperatures by 1.5° as specified in the 2015 Paris agreement. The Dubai-based Cop 28 is already being accused of being a cop out by its failure to call for phasing out the use of fossil fuels. It prefers instead the wording of compromise that, globally, we will *transition* away from them. By how much remains open to nation-by-nation interpretation. More and more talk in the relevant press seems to focus simply on holding global temperatures to their present level and managing the consequences the best we can. That's tough on you Samoa, but no one that matters will worry until Miami goes under water or the Thames rises above the London flood barrier. It seems that there has been a worldwide shrug of the shoulders and a collective wail of *There's nothing I can do.*

My answer to this lady was a suggestion that she think not in terms of what she cannot do but what she can do. I looked around for an example. *Look at this* I said taking a piece of kitchen towel from my lunchbox. It was tan in colour and far from the pristine white that we expect to see in our domestic consumable paper products. *It's unbleached, made from bamboo, grown in managed plantations. In fact,* I said, *next time I purchase, I will buy unbleached product made from recycled cardboard.*

I do this with all of my household paper consumable products – kitchen roll, facial tissues, toilet paper et cetera. It takes an adjustment because we are so used to seeing white paper. But the bleach required to make that paper pristine-white pours straight down the drain and out into the sea. How many marine environments are destroyed by our white kitchen paper every year? How many fish die? How many coral reefs? It doesn't have to be that way. We could all be using unbleached household paper but most people turn their nose up at the idea because the colour is unappealing.

So, after careful thought, I'm using this Flash to list some of the personal changes I have made in my attempt to reduce my own contribution to planetary damage. Please let me emphasise that I do this, not to signal my virtue, but to point out some of the things it is possible to do – some of the changes that are within your power if you have not already made them – to reduce the impact we all have on the planet.

Like most of us, I have made the changes that the government encourages to insulation levels and low-powered light bulbs in my home. But it's possible to go much, much further. Who decided that we need 270mm of loft insulation? This year I have installed double that level. My house is noticeably more comfortable as a result. Perhaps one of you experts out there can tell me how much carbon dioxide has been saved. How long will it take to recover the investment? I have no idea but it is undoubtedly better for our planetary home to be reducing the amount of CO_2 pumped into the air as a result of heating my own personal home.

I have also installed solar panels on my roof. I'm told it will take ten years or so to recover the cost of doing so. I don't know if I have ten years left on this planet to recover the money but that does not concern me. Like a lot people I am in a position to do this and if I want to bequeath an inhabitable planet to my grandchildren then this is not a 'nice to have' but a 'need to have'.

Okay, I get it. I am fortunate to be in the financial position to do this. Such levels of expenditure are beyond the means of many. But even if you do not have substantial resources there is still a lot you can do to contribute. For example, some time back I stopped using liquid soap and went back to buying solid bars like we all did years ago. Somewhere along the way, some advertising company had convinced me that liquid soap was superior to solid soap. I gave no thought to the packaging I was dropping into my waste bin as a result. Bars of soap also cost less than the equivalent quantity of liquid soap in the plastic container. It's a win-win. Why aren't we all doing it?

It's a similar story with shampoo. Until this year I had been in the habit of washing my hair in the shower every day, using liquid shampoo. I am now told in the numerous articles I read that I'm not doing my scalp any favours by such frequent washing. So I cut back to using shampoo just twice a week. My hair still gets wet in the shower daily, but my shampoo consumption has dropped to less than one third of what it was. Not only do all those chemicals no longer go down the drain, the plastic containers I used to discard or recycle now don't get bought in the first place. And no, I have not noticed any detrimental impact on my personal cleanliness. I hope you haven't either.

Do I really need to drive the mile into town every time I visit? A lot of the time I can go on foot – not to the point where I get soaked, or freeze my fingers off during inclement weather. But when I can walk instead of drive, I do. Similarly, where it is practical to take the train instead of using the car for longer journeys, then I do that. And next time I change my vehicle I anticipate replacing it with either an EV or a hybrid.

I could go on at considerable length but I think you get the idea.

Will this solve the problem of global warming? Clearly not. I need a bit of help from China, the USA and from you in order to do that. As I said to that dear lady, focus not on what you cannot do, because that simply takes you down the road to despair. Focus on what you can do to make a change. Come up with one change you can make today, make it and then look for the next one tomorrow. We can change the devastation we are still bringing to this planet if, collectively, we have the will to do so.

And I'll not be climbing any motorway bridges or super-gluing myself to the tarmac of London streets until I have done everything in my personal power to make the way I live as planet-friendly as possible.

What is the personal contribution you can make today, or this week or this year? Write and tell me.

49 Faggots In Gravy

On Friday, I read with some sadness of the death of Shane MacGowan of the Irish punk rock band, The Pogues. Despite having written a novel based on punk rock called *Vicious*, I was never actually a punk rocker myself. But I did take a considerable interest in what lay behind the intensity of emotion that drove so many young people of my generation to push safety pins through their cheeks and carve their hair into styles last seen on native North Americans in the nineteenth century. That was in the 1970s, when some of the better-known icons such as Sid Vicious were drawn to extremes of suicide and, though it was never proven in court, possibly drug-fuelled murder.

The only explanation I was ever able to come up with is the likelihood that such behaviour was driven by hopelessness arising from a sense of powerlessness. Were you born into poverty, relative or absolute? Did your failure in formal education push you to the margins of ridicule and exclusion? Are the prospects of finding meaningful, adequately remunerated employment non-existent? Then you find ways of expressing your anger and frustration, however odd or offensive it appears to the well-fed, well-heeled, well-satisfied conformists that look on in bemusement.

The behaviour of the few strikes a chord with the dissatisfactions of the many, so that pretty soon you have a movement, a bandwagon onto which the money-makers will always jump. A concert where musicians smash their instruments, spit on the audience and scream *f*** you* at anyone in sight? Sure, we can give you that. Buy your tickets, pay your dues. Come and enjoy hating everyone and everything that you blame, for an evening in the company of hordes of your fellow-frustrated. Then return home to whatever home might be – a middle-class, parental, halls-adjoining semi-d, an ill-maintained council house on a deprived estate, or a cardboard box in a shop doorway. Nothing has changed. Tomorrow you will get up to face the same future you fall sleep with tonight. But at least for a few hours you have felt better.

By the 1980s, the energy of Punk had to some extent been channelled and mixed with older musical traditions practised by arguably more gifted musicians. One of the results was the emergence of punk folk and one of its high priests, Shane MacGowan, fixed into the formaldehyde of memory by the song, Fairytale For New York. Indisputably tuneful and lyrical, it sustains and encapsulates the hopeless cynicism of original punk:

Christmas Day in the drunk tank makes me think of you, babe. Because I put a bet on a lucky horse that came in at 18-to-1, that's an omen that next year is definitely going to be better for both of us. Those dreams we hid for fear of them being dashed? We can share them, mingle them, until together we realise them. So we kissed in the corner and danced through the night – until, our shared dream faded and the 'you' I found myself with was no longer handsome or pretty. Now I see you as an old slut on drugs, a scumbag, a maggot, and I pray God this is our last Christmas together. You let me down. And yet I still can't leave you because I can't make it on my own. So here we remain, lost in the cycle of hopelessness and cynicism born of disappointment, too broken inside and outside to muster the will to change. And through it all, those bells are still ringing out for Christmas Day.

Much later, in the year 2000, Kirsty MacColl, Shane McGowan's co-singer on Fairytale For New York, died tragically whilst saving her teenage son in a diving accident in Mexico. Shane battled alcohol addiction all his life, stemming, it is said, from being given Guinness to drink at the age of five, to help him sleep. That was followed by a life spent professionally and personally in drinking establishments. Is it a tad ironic that before dying on the 30th of November he had accepted the administration of last rites?

Sleep soundly, Shane. And when you next wake, keep hitting those keys. You might finally make it to number one this Christmas, if we can live with your use of the word f***** but somehow I really don't think you'll give a f***.

50 A Big Ask

Some days I find myself wondering if I should give up watching and reading the news. It seems that when I switch on a TV newscast or open a newspaper on my iPad, all I see is a stream of negativity: criticisms of past failures in the COVID enquiry, shock and anger for current tragedies in Gaza, and fear for the future of an exhausted planet.

Then I stop, allow my raised heart rate to settle and begin to focus from a perspective of calm, on the suffering that I see around me. To arrive at equanimity is not callous or uncaring. To be at peace with yourself does not exclude the compassion you feel for those who are losing families in war zones, feeling resentment at their abandonment during a pandemic in which the government seemingly partied on, or facing the destruction of a life's work as a result of economic dislocation. Arriving at personal serenity and sustaining an inner condition of calm does not make me immune to the worries of the world. If anything, I feel them more. But it does place me in a more resourceful state to consider what I might be able to do practically to ease suffering, however far from or near to me it might be.

History consistently teaches us that to react by reflex in an over-animated, emotional state usually achieves no more than the salving of feelings at great cost. And it commonly leads to ineffective, if devastating, action.

Affronted by a 9/11 atrocity, you look about the world for somebody to hit back at. You bomb and march your way into Afghanistan, purportedly to eradicate Al Qaeda. Twenty years later, with thousands of lives and billions of dollars lost, you limp back out again. Everything goes back to how it was. And now you stand by mutely as women are driven out of work and education, and the population to which you gave hope sinks in despair back under the waves of ignorant oppression. You have achieved nothing lasting for the devastating price that has been paid by them and by you – 'you' of course being the populations of western nations and veterans – never 'you' as in presidents and prime ministers.

Shocked and enraged to apoplexy by a modern-day slaughter of the innocents, you bomb Gaza relentlessly to destroy Hamas once and for all. Except you can't. For every terrorist you eradicate you also kill innumerable non-combatants who simply wanted to get on with their lives.

And upon those that survive, you imprint such resentment and anger that you simply re-create the problem another generation or two on. How many ten-year-olds wandering dazed through the refugee camps of southern Gaza will, ten years from now, simply be the next generation of terrorists, hell-bent on driving the Children of Israel from the river into the sea?

Love your enemies, said Jesus. *Do good to those that hate you*.[13] It's an indescribably big ask, isn't it? At the very moment you most want to react in righteous anger and fully justified outrage, that you should look at the machine-gun propped up in the corner, that you should look at the hotline to the head of the armed forces, and not pick them up; that when the urge is strongest to retaliate, to eradicate a clear threat, to demolish an obvious danger, you stop and first find equanimity. And then, having found it, you ask yourself what it is that has caused human beings to react in an inhuman way. And you determine that making sure it never happens again means not flattening your neighbour's cities and putting their children into coffins but discovering why they are driven to murder and atrocities from which neither you nor they will ever recover.

Greek mythology tells of the Furies, goddesses of anger, jealousy and revenge, who perpetuated a cycle of hatred caused by misdeeds and atrocities. For each act of effrontery, they drove the wronged one or their representatives to exact a terrible retribution on the perpetrator or his loved ones. On and on the cycle continued, demanding an eye for an eye, a tooth for a tooth or preferably two eyes or teeth for one. Only then was honour restored. Only then was justice served. And then, of course, the one who had lost two eyes, or two teeth, had long forgotten the original cause and was driven to exact their own revenge.

More than two thousand years later, we eschew the language of revenge. Now we talk of eradicating threats, keeping our populations safe, ensuring the unthinkable is not permitted to happen again. But each night a bomb is dropped or a knife wielded, slaying someone's son, someone's grandmother, someone's baby, each night the Furies return to whisper words of revenge in the ears of the grief-wracked. And each morning they arise once more to a world emptied of what they loved, their hearts filled with hatred, until later, sometimes much, much later, they too stalk the darkness in pursuit of revenge.

Bless them that curse you, do good to them that hate you, and pray for them which despitefully use you[14] It is a big ask indeed, but if we do not rise to its call, then all we do is stand back and watch, as Gandhi put it, while the demanding of an eye for an eye makes the whole world blind.

51 Role Over, Clint

I am back on Tenerife to complete this book. This morning, I have driven a few kilometres to the inelegantly named Golf del Sur, intending to walk to the adjacent village of Los Abrigos. There, the plan is to sit at a table outside my favourite café, La Dulce, to write while enjoying a coffee and croissant. Though I knew I wanted to write, it wasn't until I got into the car that the subject descended on me: Dallas. Not the city, you understand, but the TV programme that started in the 1970s.

I find a parking space behind the imposing, Hotel Vincci that stands at the very eastern corner of 'the Golf,' its rooms staring proudly out East, South and West, over the sparkling Atlantic Ocean. Tenerife lies just 4° North of the Tropic of Cancer and 300 km from the African Coast. Except at the height of its very hot summers, the climate is like unending spring.

I take the steps down from the hotel to the boardwalk that follows the shoreline for a kilometre or so, dipping down to the level of the sea then rising back up as you approach the fishing village of Los Abrigos. The boardwalk was completed in 2020. Before that, the intrepid would clamber over the rocks and up steep slopes in pursuit of a fish supper at one of the many restaurants that line the sloping promenade that leads down to the harbour. At the tables of the most desirable of them, you can sit and look directly out into the sunset, while the chefs cook your choice from the chilled cabinet. It's all today's catch, as the fishing boats bobbing up and down in front of the restaurant remind you. And yes, we did it many times before I embraced vegetarian eating in 2017 – though we mostly drove to the village in preference to the somewhat hazardous scramble over the rocks.

The 350 episodes of Dallas were screened in the UK for thirteen years from 1978 onwards. To sit in front of it was an act of family worship orchestrated by my father. Speaking, or even shuffling, was sacrilege to rival talking in church. No disturbance was permitted as he released his inner JR Ewing, an ethereal Stetson hovering just above his head. The rest of us found it a bit of a giggle, truth to tell. Only later did I come to realise what a role model JR had been for him. How much the power wielded by such a man appealed to those who found their powerlessness emasculating.

Thirty years before that, it was Paul Henreid who lit two cigarettes simultaneously in the movie, Now Voyager, passing one to Betty Davis who hesitated for but a moment before displaying traditional female acquiescence to the alpha male in accepting it. Everyone tried to do it after that. All the men wanted to be as effortlessly self-assured around women as Paul was. Plenty came close to self-immolation in the fumbled pursuit of imaged power. Ten years after that, young men stood in front of mirrors, their black-dyed hair slicked back with industrial quantities of Brylcreem, desperately trying to achieve that elusive Elvis quiff, as they snarled at their images in doomed attempts to become more admirable.

Crossing a little wooden bridge at sea level, I happen upon an enterprising and somewhat elderly Spanish lady who is sitting in the sunshine, crocheting babies' bootees. Ten pairs or so are lined up on the ground in front of her. I ask permission to take her picture and in doing so notice the crutches propped up on the back of her chair. Her body may be failing but her spirit is indomitable. She crochets to make her life better – from a little more cash and a considerable amount of self-esteem that emanates from doing something useful. And she does it to create joy. Her slippers will light up the face of a passing child. An indulgent mum or dad will hand over €10 and smile as they make their baby happy.

Round about the time my father was dreaming of

an invitation to the Oil Barons' ball, I was preoccupied with converting the undergraduate population of Oxford University to my preferred and very charismatic interpretation of Christianity. I was more than surprised when my close and similarly-minded friend Chris disclosed a secret admiration for Kojak. This blunt-talking New York detective managed to rack up a mere 118 episodes from 1973 to 1978, beating up bad guys but never quite beating his smoking addiction with his trademark lollipop sucking. Chris never went as far as shaving his head but the attraction to the dominant male role was undeniable even for one whose prime preoccupation was to emulate Jesus.

The boardwalk begins to rise up with the cliff about half way across. A shapely young lady, dressed in the shortest of cut-off shorts, glides past me on a silent electric scooter and disappears. When I round the bend at the top of the rise I happen upon a wider boarded area, where a dozen or so equally shapely young people of both sexes are practicing yoga stretches under the watchful eye of a teacher who is holding a smartphone. I am not tempted to join them. I know from my feeble attempts at chair yoga in the privacy of my own apartment just how inflexible my limbs have become. My mind, I hope, still flexes reasonably well. But I have to admit that over the years I have treated it with more care than I have my body.

My own preferred brand of role model in my twenties

was Clint Eastwood. Which of his characters, you ask? Well, all of them really, since for most of his acting career he played only one – the silent, hard-to-provoke cowboy/cop/soldier of infrequent words who felt no need to display his power. Somehow he always managed to find himself in the midst of trouble, where he would be called upon to save the town, the country, or the planet. Only in his later years did he graduate to the deeper roles of Unforgiven and Grand Torino. But he was my hero, and I would accept no other. I, too, wanted that subtle, undeclared power that ran deep, appearing only when it was time to save weaker mortals.

Arriving at Los Abrigos, I find all the tables at La Dulce occupied – January is high season on Tenerife and by 10.30am the café culture is throbbing. I'll need to arrive earlier next time. I wander down to the harbour in the hope of finding somewhere to sip a coffee and write. But all the restaurants here open only from lunchtime to late evening and they make their money from bigger spenders than me. No one wants to serve coffee in these high-overhead establishments. At the bottom of the slope I watch, entranced, as a solitary crab makes a bid for freedom from the holding tanks of Restaurante Los Abrigos. She scuttles to the edge of the quay then takes a leap down into the dark waters that lap a couple of meters below. I'm glad she has escaped. I'm glad she's not going to get eaten today. But I can't feel any ill-will towards the fishermen who make their living catching her fellows, nor the restaurant staff who make theirs from serving crabs in their shells to tourists as the sun drops down into the sea. It's a difficult world for the gentle to reconcile.

Sometime in the present century, I appeared to have become something of a role model myself, albeit in a rather modest way. Business people and spiritual people at different times spontaneously told me I was an inspiration. I was glad, though I hope not in an egotistical way. Finally, in about 2018, I found myself standing on a stage in front of five hundred or so university students. *How can we be more like you?* came the question, so overtly put that this time I could not avoid the issue. I groaned inwardly, knowing they were looking at an image, not seeing the reality of the man. Larry Hagman, Telly Savalas, Clint Eastwood – they all stripped off their screen personas when they walked off set. They all went home to live in the realities of family, ill-considered decisions, health issues - challenges of the same kind that you and I face. *Believe me,* I answered, painfully aware of my own failings and problems, *you do not want to be more like me. But what you can be and what I want for you is to become the very best version of yourself that you can.*

I make my way back up the slope and check on my favoured café once more but all the tables are still occupied, both inside and out. So I head back over the boardwalk, thinking about how my role models, my image of what it is to be a worthy man, have changed over the years. The movie and TV actors of my twenties gave way to successful businessmen like Sir Richard Branson in my thirties, and were replaced in my forties by the spiritually aware such as Wayne Dyer. Now I learn from many, but seek to emulate none. Somewhere along the boardwalk of life, I realised that role models just play roles and do that only for a short time. I no longer want to be a role player or a role seeker. All I want is to walk in the light.

52 When To Stop

'You tell me when to stop,' says Jacqui. We are both settling down to Writing Practice in Costa for our agreed 20-minute period. Twenty minutes seems long enough for me to let go and let it happen – for spirit to take my hand, you might say, if you are spiritually inclined. So the process starts and I discipline myself to keep the pen moving as it is supposed to.

Then the thoughts of self-doubt that are familiar to me begin to flow. *This won't go anywhere. This really isn't all that good. It's not up to your usual standard.* And now that I am approaching the end of the book: *You've wasted your time. No one will want to read this. It's a pointless, nothing book. Even if the people close to you say positive things about it, that's only because they are trying to be kind, to ensure you are not upset, not disappointed. But a real, paid-up card-carrying spiritual book that will touch hearts and illuminate journeys? You? Who do you think you are, you charlatan?*

I've heard it all before of course. But though this is my eleventh book, the messages of self-doubt continue to filter through as much as they always did. I guess they always will. And I want you to know that they do because I'm guessing that you too are filled with doubt about yourself from time to time. Perhaps we all are. Perhaps that is the nature of the human condition.

So what do we need to do when we are engaged in a project, or on a journey of exploration, seeking light and find that the doubt sets in, distracting us, trying to persuade us to drop the whole thing? My only answer is that you bat on regardless of how you feel.

Zen teaches me that a thought is just a thought, an emotion just a feeling. They puff themselves up, disguise themselves as powerful when they are not. The power of feelings and thoughts to harm us comes only from the belief that we choose to invest in them. Have the courage, just once, to get up and walk away from them and you find that you smash through them, leaving them to evaporate and return to the emptiness from which they first arose. And that single act can be enough to teach you that you are the powerful one, that you have everything it takes to achieve your life purpose to overcome, to learn and grow.

May we be powerful and courageous today, both you

and I, when we confront our dragons. May we overcome and discover how weak and powerless they really are.

And now I really must go. It is time for me to tell Jacqui to stop writing.

Acknowledgements

I want to express my deep gratitude to my editors, Jacqueline Haskell and Susan Aldworth for their enormous support and assistance in the creation of this book. It quite simply would not have come into being without their continued encouragement, patience, constructive criticism, and many hours of editorial and proofreading work. I claim exclusive ownership of all remaining errors.

References

1   For further information concerning Henry Shukman see https://henryshukman.com/

2   For further information concerning Natalie Goldberg see https://nataliegoldberg.com/

3   *Writing Down The Bones*, Natalie Goldberg Second (Expanded) Edition Shambhala 2002

4   *The True Secret of Writing*, Natalie Goldberg Atria 2014

5   https://www.mantakchia.com/

6   https://www.wakingup.com/

7   I'll Sleep When I'm Dead 2003 directed by Mike Hodges

8   *The Great Failure*, Natalie Goldberg HarperOne Reprinted 2025

9   A Great Wagon, Rumi
    https://onbeing.org/poetry/a-great-wagon/

10 *Ode on a Grecian Urn*, John Keats (1795-1821) 1816

11 *If*, Rudyard Kipling (1865-1936) c 1895

12   *Stroking Cerberus,* Jacqueline Haskell Myriad Editions
     2020
     Stroking Cerberus was published as part of the Spotlight
     Books collaboration between Creative Future, New
     Writing South and Myriad Editions to discover, guide
     and support writers who are under-represented due to
     mental or physical health issues, disability, race, class,
     gender identity or social circumstance.
13   Bible, Luke 6:27 KJV
14   Bible, Luke 6:28 KJV

Resources

Thich Nhat Hanh *The Heart of the Buddha's Teaching* Rider, 1999

The Miracle of Mindfulness, Rider, 2008

Pema Chodron, *Welcoming the Unwelcome* Shambhala, 2019

Henry Shukman, *One Blade of Grass – A Zen Memoir* Counterpoint Press, 2019

Yongey Mingyur Rinpoche, *Turning Confusion Into Clarity* Shambhala, 2014

Sam Harris, *Book: Waking Up* Bantam, 2014

Website: www.waking up.com

Shunryu Suzuki, *Zen Mind, Beginner's Mind* Shambhala, 1970

Biographical

Image by Minnie Harding

Michael Forester writes at the fulcrum of perceived reality. His works range from the inspirational and provocative *Forest Rain* to the book-length metaphorical epic poem *Dragonsong*; from his exploration of our endangered planet in the travelogue *One Journey;* to the ever-popular story of his first year with his hearing dog, Matt, *If It Wasn't For That Dog*.

His books are followed worldwide, from Australia to California, from the Philippines to Wales. A profoundly deaf full-time author and public speaker, Michael is 68 years old. He lives in the UK between the southern edge of the New Forest and the sea from where he travels internationally to speak publicly and sign his books for readers.

Michael's own life journey has taken him from formative years in charismatic Christianity, through a miraculously survived suicide attempt and into a spiritual awakening, through the onset of profound deafness and the life-changing arrival of a hearing dog. He has travelled the planet from the Amazon rainforest to South Africa, from the Himalayas to the Philippines and beyond.

Michael Forester's books are available at his website **www.michaelforester.co.uk** and on Amazon. To order signed copies of Michael's books or request speaking engagements email **michaelforesterauthor@gmail.com**

Other Books by Michael Forester

**All Michael Forester's books are available via
Michaelforester.co.uk**

This unique collection of essays, metaphors and verse has
been called one of the great books of all time, a book that
will open doors in your heart and mind. Here, you will
find:

• The soul awakening that follows
a near death experience

• The unseen protectors who are
always about us, guiding our life
journey

• The love we pursue relentlessly
until we realise that it was always
seeking us

Forest Rain will lead you on a journey into your own
soul, to face your fears, your regrets and your life purpose
and so to find the love that has always awaited you.

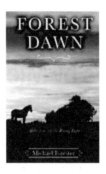

In this, his second collection of inspirational essays, metaphors and poetry, Michael Forester illuminates the profound that hides in the simple and the eternal that shines through the commonplace.

A man tries to buy peace by the pound... a child learns the transience of life when he treads on a spider... angels appear just when needed.

Here, we encounter the healing power of our dreams and the lessons that dancing holds for life's journey... a life-changing confrontation with a beggar... what we find because of what we lose.

Forest Dawn will make you laugh and it will make you cry. But most of all, it will bring you face-to-face with the person who can teach you most: yourself.

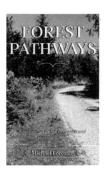

This is the third book in Michael Forester's much loved series of essays, metaphorical stories and poetry inspired by walks of solitude in England's New Forest and beyond.

Journey with Michael and his beloved hearing dog, Matt, into the deeper places, where the snowmelt cascades from your soul, where water whispers its own story and gold belongs only to the moon. Take a risk and read *The Story That Changes Your Future* to discover the future that you always wanted but never knew was already yours.

Here you will discover a man who seeks the right way to Live – the town called Live, that is; a *ménage à trois* in which the lovers are named Enlightenment and Ambition; a road that leads to the land of the Sun.

Forest Pathways pours out metaphor after metaphor, insight after insight, leading you on a rising, winding pathway that takes you deeper into the Forest of your own heart and beyond.

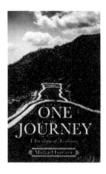

There is only One Journey. We commence it the moment we enter the physical world and complete it the moment we leave. Our journey is travelled on a road of self-discovery. During that journey, we may take many trips, make many voyages. Here are four, undertaken over a period of fourteen years:

In the Amazon rainforest, a confrontation with the unceasing exploitation of its resources and people.

In South Africa, an encounter with the power of forgiveness, fifteen years after the ending of apartheid.

In Nepal and the Himalayas, a pilgrimage of self-discovery.

In the Philippines, an exploration of the impact of economic modernisation upon the people and the land.

Each explores how, if we have the eyes to see and the ears to hear, our voyages into the world are, in reality, a reflection of our journey into ourselves.

It's amazing what you can achieve with persistence, a bit of chopped liver and a second hand teddy bear....

In 2002 Michael, a deafened man from the New Forest, lost his home, his marriage, his business and his father – but he can't actually remember if it was in that order. However, in the same year someone suggested that getting a dog might be a good idea – not just any dog, but a hearing dog from Hearing Dogs for Deaf People. And when, in 2004, Michael was presented with a hearing dog of his own called Matt, he just *knew* life would be so much easier. Amazing how wrong you can be, isn't it!

If It Wasn't For That Dog is the story of Matt's first year with Michael, the challenges and accomplishments of climbing the hearing-dog learning curve, the profound changes he stimulated and the inestimable joy he confers magically on everyone who meets him. But most of all it is the story of the strange power of meaty treats to work miracles in doggie behaviour.

Rebekah, daughter of Merlin and noblewoman of Albion, has been driven to madness by the murder of her lover, Vidar. In her torment she bargains with the Prince of Demons to turn her into a dragon. Once so transformed, she seeks to take revenge upon her father, Merlin, for she has been fooled into believing he is responsible for Vidar's death. Behind the subterfuge stands Oberon, Captain-King of Elves, who cannot foresee the devastation his jealousy and unrequited love for Rebekah will unleash upon the world of Gaia. Its salvation depends upon the retrieval of the Sleep Stone from the gates of Hell. But if the stone is not returned, the demon army will awaken and ransack Gaia in a war that will destroy it. Time is the solution – but only if the gods of Asgard can find a way of stopping it.

Well hello there.

Why don't you step inside and take a look round? You remember this place, don't you? That's right. You've been here before. And us. Surely you remember us. We're old friends. This is where the light in your eyes glimpses the darkness in your mind. Sit down and stay a while – if you can face the risk, that is.

I'll introduce you to some friends of mine:

Come meet the man who remembers his birth. He wishes he didn't. And the goblin child – if his mother is to be believed, that is. Or how about the boy who takes his god to school? And Santa. You really wouldn't want to leave without meeting Santa, would you? But really it's all about David, you understand, who spent his life circling the moon – just like you and I do, in fact. Come with me. Come with me now.

It's 2117 in a country where everything you do has to be approved by the state; a state that tells you what to eat, when to shower, when to make love, what to think. As the waters rise in the city, the fish people begin to arrive. Utterly compliant, they open and close their mouths incessantly, saying nothing. When Greg dares to think for himself, the Departmental Republic seeks to draw him into their elite to keep him quiet. But if he agrees, it's going to cost him his home and the life of his family.

For thirty years, Tolly's been waiting for the reincarnation of rock star Sid Vicious who's definitely coming back to love her forever. Now that she's certain she's found him in the form of young Henry, well, Henry's girlfriend Laura has to be stalked and eliminated, doesn't she?

But... something's not right. Because when Tolly kidnaps Laura, hovering in the background are unearthly wispy creatures – *Ethereals*, they call themselves. Is this some kind of a game?

Could Laura really be miraculously pregnant with the second coming of the Messiah, as her Pastor, Philemon Littlemann insists? Or is she just as insane as Tolly?

Too: the sequel to *Vicious*

What do you do when your daughter is murdered during childbirth?

What do you do when you're told your grandchild is the second coming of The Messiah?

What do you do when powerful forces seek to take that child to exploit it?

What do you do when you alone know the secret the child carries that proves its divinity?

What do you do?

You run.